Everyday
Snack Tray

Everyday Snack Tray

Easy Ideas and Recipes for Boards That Nourish for Moments Big and Small

FRANCES LARGEMAN-ROTH, RDN

Revell

a division of Baker Publishing Group
Grand Rapids, Michigan

© 2023 by Milk & Honey Media, LLC

Published by Revell
a division of Baker Publishing Group
Grand Rapids, Michigan
www.revellbooks.com

Printed in China

Library of Congress Cataloging-in-Publication Data
Names: Largeman-Roth, Frances, author. | Volo, Lauren, photographer.
Title: Everyday snack tray : easy ideas and recipes for boards that nourish for moments big and small / Frances Largeman-Roth, RDN ; photographs by Lauren Volo.
Description: Grand Rapids : Revell, a division of Baker Publishing Group, [2023] | Includes index.
Identifiers: LCCN 2022050912 | ISBN 9780800744991 (cloth) | ISBN 9781493443567 (ebook)
Subjects: LCSH: Snack foods. | Seasonal cooking. | Holiday cooking. | LCGFT: Cookbooks.
Classification: LCC TX740 .L327 2023 | DDC 641.5/3—dc23/eng/20221121
LC record available at https://lccn.loc.gov/2022050912

Photography by Lauren Volo

Food styling by Mira Evnine

Prop styling by Maeve Sheridan

Interior design by Jane Klein

This publication is intended to provide helpful and informative material on the subjects addressed. Readers should consult their personal health professionals before adopting any of the suggestions in this book or drawing inferences from it. The author and publisher expressly disclaim responsibility for any adverse effects arising from the use or application of the information contained in this book.

The proprietor is represented by the literary agency of Stoker Literary, Inc.

Baker Publishing Group publications use paper produced from sustainable forestry practices and post-consumer waste whenever possible.

23 24 25 26 27 28 29   7 6 5 4 3 2 1

To Willa, Leo, and Phoebe for providing me with a steady stream of inspiration and motivation. I also appreciate you putting up with my deadlines, and for being such amazing—and honest—recipe testers. And to Jon for always making me feel like my dreams are tangible, and for sharing this wild ride with me. I love you all so much!

Contents

EVERYDAY SNACK TRAYS

winter

spring

summer

fall

Introduction

People often assume that mealtime at my house is perfectly balanced and effortless since I am a registered dietitian and cookbook author. Sure, I strive for nutritious and well-made meals—but honestly, I'm often too busy or too tired to cook. Plus, my husband, Jon, and I have three very different kids with very different palates and food preferences. Willa, our oldest, doesn't eat meat and has a sensitive palate (things often just taste "weird" to her). Leo eats pretty much everything—usually. And Phoebe, our youngest, has a healthy appetite but a limited selection of foods she enjoys.

Pulling off nutritious meals each night—especially when our kids were younger—felt nearly impossible. Out of desperation, I started to serve little bits of food in small ramekins—primarily so that food wouldn't go to waste. But I found that my three kids (and husband) responded well to this snacky, "tapas" style of food presentation, and it made them more willing to try new things. The best part—it was much less work for me!

Fast-forward a year or so, and my kids started asking for snack trays for their birthdays and on weekends. I realized not only that I enjoyed putting them together but also that it was a low-stress way to introduce new and different foods to my kids. Instead of piling their plates with various

> Putting together snack trays was a low-stress way to introduce new and different foods to my kids.

veggies, I could let them be curious and take small amounts to try at their own pace. And while there may not always be enough grilled shrimp or other protein left over for a full meal, it is often just the right amount to present on a tray.

As a working mom who doesn't always have time to make the perfect meal or decorate a special cake, I find trays and boards to be a way to creatively celebrate holidays and special times. I can make something from scratch, such as waffles, dips, latkes, or cookies, and combine it with fresh fruit, veggies, and store-bought items to create an inviting selection of nibbles.

If you're looking for tips on making the perfect salami rose for your char-cuterie, *Everyday Snack Tray* isn't for you. But if you're looking for simple, accessible ideas to put together a board that looks inviting and will impress the neighbors' kids as well as your own, you've come to the right place.

Each snack tray includes just one from-scratch recipe, such as No-Bake Cereal Bars, Buffalo Cauliflower Bites, Mini Dragon Fruit and Chia Puddings, Peppermint Whipped Cream, or Classic Creamy Hummus. Many of the recipes offer a vegan option so that everyone can enjoy them. Don't have time to make something? All the recipes are optional. Every board can be executed without them and still look fab!

Everyday snack trays are for the parents and caretakers who want to make their kids' day a little brighter or that holiday morning extra special but who might not be the best cooks or food stylists in the world. I hope you'll feel inspired by this book and that it will help you create memories you and your family will cherish forever. Taking the stress out of food prep is the best way to celebrate!

These trays don't require any particular expertise, but you can add all the flair you want! Life is busy and complicated, and nothing here is any more difficult than something you can put together on a weeknight. I hope that *Everyday Snack Tray* gives you more reasons to gather with loved ones and sit at the table just a bit longer.

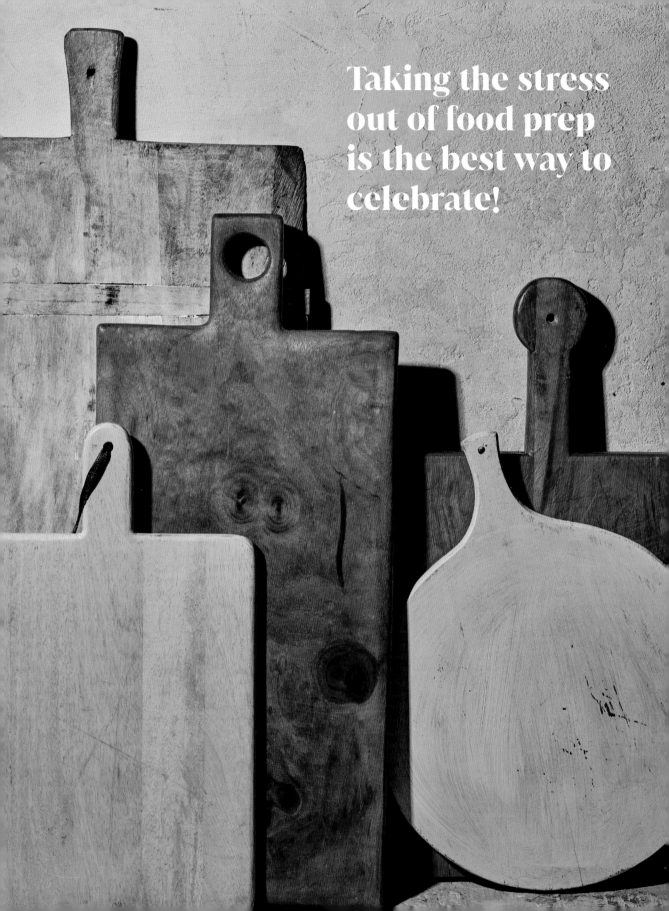

Taking the stress out of food prep is the best way to celebrate!

1

THE RULES OF SNACK TRAYS

THERE ARE NO RULES!

You can put a tray or board together with whatever sounds delicious to you. Even though you'll see themed boards in this book, your boards can be *anything* you want them to be—they don't have to be themed *or* fancy at all. But I do have visual suggestions that will help your trays look beautiful and purposeful.

- **Make a pattern.** This works especially well when you have lots of smallish items, like mini cupcakes or cut-up pieces of fruit, as with the Valentine's Day Tray on page 54. A round tray lends itself to organizing food in concentric circles, while alternating rows of food look great on a rectangular or square tray.

- **Vary your heights.** I remember my high school drama teacher, Mr. Ferrara, telling us sets look more interesting when there are props of different heights on the stage. The same holds true for boards. It's fun to see a tall glass full of straws rising up from a tray that's otherwise flat. You can always add height by putting an upside-down ramekin under a small plate on your tray like we did with the Fall Fest Tray on page 158.

- **Delight the senses.** A one-note tray isn't very compelling, just like a closet full of only black dresses isn't very exciting. Think about

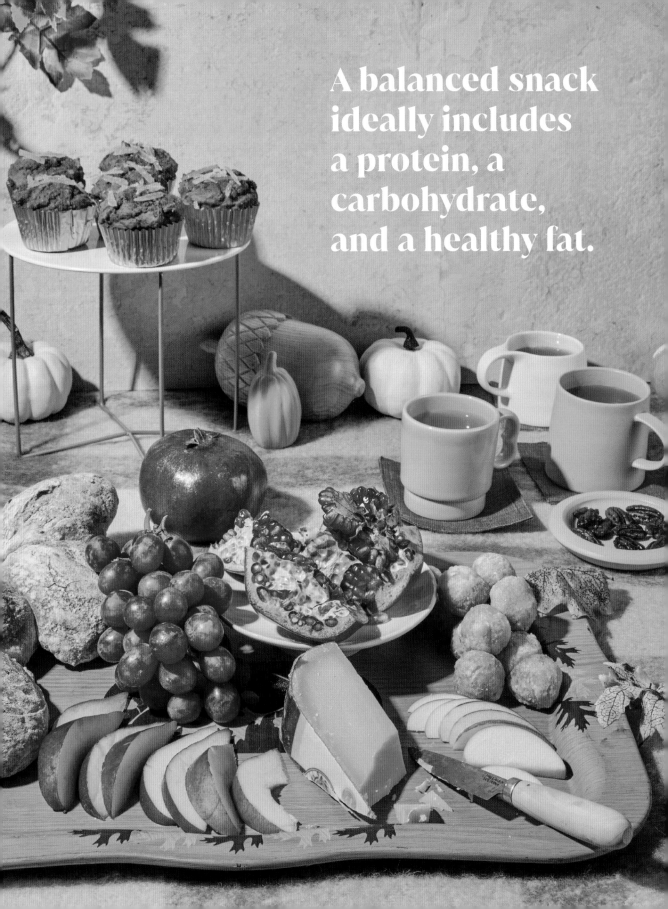

A balanced snack ideally includes a protein, a carbohydrate, and a healthy fat.

including creamy items along with crunchy, and something sweet to balance spicy flavors. Keep all the senses in mind when you're putting your trays together, and they'll be sure to captivate.

- **Abundance is always good.** Boards should look plentiful, not skimpy. But that doesn't mean you need to fill your board with piles of expensive things. For example, covering your board in aged cheese and prosciutto isn't necessary, but you can certainly be bountiful with tortilla chips, baby carrots, graham crackers, and other less pricey items. And boards made for one don't need to be as saturated, but they should still look generous!

- **Choose a color scheme.** Even if all the foods are of different types, you can still make a tray look pulled together by choosing a single color or color scheme. I made a black-and-white tray when the latest Cruella movie came out. The food ranged in type from licorice to ravioli, but the fact that the color scheme ran through everything made it visually appealing.

- **Keep it bite-size.** Since snack trays are for doing just that, food should be served in a nibble-able form. For example, it's fine to place a block of cheese on your board, but slice several pieces and leave a cheese knife handy so anyone can slice more when needed. Cut fruits or vegetables into pieces that can be easily snacked on or picked up with a toothpick.

I'm often asked what the difference is between a snack and a meal. The nutritionist in me will say that a snack is a small combination of foods that is meant to provide energy between meals. Kids generally need a snack between breakfast and lunch and then again between lunch and dinner. A balanced snack ideally includes a protein, a carbohydrate, and a healthy fat. That combo could be cheese, crackers, and nuts or edamame, sesame sticks, and avocado.

If you're using snack trays as true snacks, you can always downsize them and include only what makes sense for you. Conversely, if you're looking to make a meal out of them, you can add additional items or go for the heartier trays like the Meatless Monday Tray (p. 152), Snow Day Tray (p. 58), Labor Day Tray (p. 118), Date Night Mezze Platter (p. 122), or Breakfast for Dinner Platter (p. 160). *You* are in the driver's seat regarding how much food to prepare and present on your tray.

2

TOOLS OF THE TRADE

EVERYTHING YOU NEED TO START MAKING FUN BOARDS AND TRAYS TODAY

One of my favorite things about snack trays is our principle from the last chapter—that there are *no* actual rules. This means I can get as creative and resourceful as I want when putting my boards together. In this chapter, we'll discuss items you may need or want for your own snack tray creations. But this process doesn't have to be fancy or expensive. Use your mugs, your small Tupperware containers that got shoved in a cupboard corner, or the random kitschy shot or tasting glasses you got "that one time" that aren't used often (or ever). This is their moment to shine.

Finding the Right Trays for You

If you have a medium-to-large tray of any kind (a wooden board, a baking sheet, even a pizza peel) and a few small bowls, you can start making trays right this minute! Of course, once you really get into it, you may want to branch out and collect an assortment of trays in various sizes and shapes, ranging from circular to rectangular.

Thanks to the rise in popularity of charcuterie and snack trays, you can now find a plethora of styles to choose from. I like the really large ones (at least

twelve inches in diameter—or closer to twenty, if I'm being honest) because they give me more room to play, but it's great to have an assortment. If you start shopping for trays, you'll find that they can come in a ton of shapes to suit every holiday—from stars to hearts to trees. Shaped trays don't hold as much, but they're a fun way to enhance a theme, and they look great on a buffet with other food.

I've been asked how I avoid messes when little hands are grabbing various foods from a tray. I actually find that serving different foods on one tray is a much neater way to share food than serving from multiple platters. My secret? I line the trays with parchment paper first, then add the various bowls and plates to it. That way, any spills are caught by the parchment, not the wood or marble surface of the tray. Lining the trays also allows me to place items like cheese and crackers directly on the surface of the tray without needing a vessel for each. And once we're done noshing, I simply remove the bowls, gather up the parchment, and toss it in the trash. It's easy cleanup, and my trays stay in great shape! I also have a couple of metal trays that I use to serve items that are extra messy, like burgers, tacos, and soup.

Another way to protect your trays from greasy or sticky foods is to do what I call "tray on tray." I use a small plate or wooden board to hold cheese or sandwiches on a larger board. You can see this technique in action on the Fourth of July Tray on page 112 and on the Breakfast for Dinner Platter on page 160. And since snack boards and trays have become so popular, you can now find trays that come with ceramic dishes that can be arranged on the tray. I have one of these from Mark and Graham, and it's wonderful for putting together a quick board that looks cohesive.

Also, if you have similarly sized trays, you can double your surface area and use them side by side like I did with the Taco Night Tray on page 96 and the New Year's Eve Party Platter on page 50. Just because you're serving food on a tray, it doesn't mean that *everything* needs to fit on just one.

I actually find that serving different foods on one tray is a much neater way to share food than serving from multiple platters.

Turning Household Items into Snack Tray Magic

Friends always ask me where I find the little ramekins and bowls I use to make my snack trays. The truth is that I'm a little bit of a magpie (my husband says I have hoarding tendencies), and I gather up things that I think will look cute on a tray. I sometimes buy a certain brand of fancy yogurt or pudding that comes in colorful ceramic pots, which I wash and keep. I also have a few sets of prep bowls, which are wide and perfect for olives, candies, and dips. And when I go shopping, I look for interesting small bowls that will look pretty on a tray. The great thing is that you can use them for anything in your home—from serving pumpkin seeds to storing jewelry.

Many items you likely already have on hand—mugs, cups, and saucers—are perfect for holding various snacks. Shot glasses can be used for mini smoothies and individual dips. Even paper or silicone cupcake liners can be used to hold small items like nuts, berries, or chocolates. Look around your kitchen and pantry and get creative!

If you are into canning or making overnight oats, you likely have lots of glass jars on hand. These can be used to hold tall items like breadsticks, celery, or cucumber spears. And I'm always scouring Target, Marshalls, TJ Maxx, Crate & Barrel, and West Elm for interesting vessels that might work on a tray. Of course, tag sales and antique stores can also be a treasure trove for fun things like tiny spoons and bowls. Just make sure to ask if the items are food safe.

And if you're looking for something very specific, like a tray in the shape of your child's first initial or letter trays to spell out your last name, you can special order virtually anything on Etsy or Zazzle. Etsy is where I found the pink letter *B* for the Baby Shower Platter on page 104. Just be sure to order things well in advance of your special celebration.

Where to Find Snack Tray Supplies

Since I often make color-themed trays, I find myself looking for specific items, like red chips or blue candies. I always scour my local grocery stores first, but if I can't find what I'm looking for, my backup is usually Amazon or Target. Some items, like M&M's and other candies, generally last a long time when stored in a cool place, so you can use them again and again. I've also had good luck finding specialty foods at Marshalls. They have items designed for bridal showers and birthday parties that originally went for top dollar at major markdowns. Score!

One of my favorite snack tray moves is to use cookie cutters to create shapes from fruit, cheese, and more. I have a large collection, and I'm always adding to it. Alphabet cookie cutters are a fun way to add a personal touch to trays (see the First Day of School Snack Tray on p. 136). Cookie cutters can also be placed directly on a tray and filled with small items, like raisins or chocolate chips. Go for at least a three-inch cutter or it won't show up very well on the tray. You can find a wide variety of cutters from stores such as Williams-Sonoma, Sur La Table, and of course Amazon.

Other Helpful Tools

Once you begin making snack trays, you'll find new uses for things all the time. One summer when I was making fruit skewers, I realized my skewers were way too long to fit on my tray. I knew scissors wouldn't work on wooden skewers, but then I thought, "Hey, what about gardening shears?" And yes, they worked perfectly!

Toothpicks also come in handy for making smaller skewers, like the ones on the New Year's Eve Party Platter on page 50. And since the spoons and forks you use for meals will likely be too large to use as serving utensils on a tray, it's nice to keep petite versions handy. A melon baller or an ice cream scoop is also a must-have tool for certain trays, like the Spooky Halloween Spread on page 138.

Also, if you haven't already invested in a great pizza wheel, do it now. You can use it to cut puff pastry for Black Sesame Parmesan Twists (recipe on p. 50), to trim the crusts from sandwiches, and to cut pizza into wedges like I did for the Neighbors Are Coming Tray on page 150.

> Once you begin making snack trays, you'll find new uses for things all the time.

3

SNACK TRAYS AS GIFTS

DITCH PRICEY PREMADE BOARDS FOR A HOMEMADE TRAY

Boards and trays have become popular items to give as gifts or to order when you're hosting gatherings. But the price tags on many of them are hefty—with some topping $300! Once you become adept at putting together trays, you'll probably start getting requests to bring them to parties—trust me! And they make lovely gifts for friends, especially if you're giving them the tray that you're presenting the food on.

Assembling and Transporting Trays

Because so many elements go on trays, they can be tricky to transport once they're composed. That's why it's easier and safer to bring all your items (cheese, crackers, fruit, etc.) in their original packaging to a gathering and then assemble everything once you arrive. Sometimes I do a "dress rehearsal" of my items while they're still in the packages so I can see generally where things will go and so I can make sure I have enough of each item. If you want to be really slick, you can precut your parchment paper liner and mark with a pencil where each item will go.

Once you become adept at putting together trays, you'll probably start getting requests to bring them to parties—trust me!

A Few of Their Favorite Things

"What would they want?" That's a terrific thought-starter when you're planning a special tray for someone. And yet . . . you might end up hearing more crickets in your brain than quick answers. Here are some tried-and-true items I've found to be a strong starting place if I'm stumped.

- Good chocolate
- Nuts (if there are no allergies)
- Quality crackers (I'm a big fan of the fruit-and-nut-studded Raincoast Crisps.)
- Cheese (You can choose ones from their favorite country or state.)
- Sweet or savory jam
- Fresh seasonal veggies and fruit
- A personalized note or memento

If you are going to bring a tray to someone as a gift, I recommend reaching out to them (or someone close to them if it's a surprise) in advance to see if there are any food allergies or preferences you should be aware of. That way you can either avoid certain ingredients altogether or make two versions of an item and label them clearly using small chalkboard signs.

Adding Nonfood Items

When you have a little extra time, sometimes it's nice to set the mood with the addition of a candle or a small flower-filled vase. Since hands and open flames aren't a great mix, I like using flameless candles. Sometimes you can find little flameless candles in fun shapes, like pumpkins or pinecones, in addition to traditional votives and pillars.

Flowers can add a special touch to a board—when it's a gift and when it's not!—especially when they match the theme of the board. If mom's favorite flowers are peonies (hint, hint), then add a bloom to her Mother's Day Breakfast-in-Bed Tray (p. 86). Or make a Date Night Mezze Platter (p. 122) look a little more fabulous with a small jar of dahlias or ranunculus—and add a little romantic glow to that one with a votive!

4

KEEPING FOOD SAFE
TAKING CARE OF PERISHABLE ITEMS

I wouldn't be doing my job as a dietitian if I didn't include some basics about food safety. It's easy to lose track of time when you're serving a tray either on a normal busy day for your family or at a larger gathering. Many of the foods you'll be putting on snack trays are fine to leave out—like chips, crackers, nuts, or candy—because they're nonperishable. But foods like dips, meats, cheeses, or other foods that contain dairy can spoil and cause foodborne illness such as salmonella, so you need to follow the two-hour rule: Perishable foods should be thrown away after they've been out for two hours. If you're serving a tray outside and the temperature is above 90°F, perishables will last only one hour.

Keep cold foods in the refrigerator until it's time to serve them. Likewise, keep hot foods, like chili or egg dishes, at 140°F or hotter until you serve them. The danger zone for perishable foods is between 40 and 140°F. Use a food thermometer, inserted into the thickest part, to check the temperature.

You might wonder if you can save food that has been on a snack tray. Yes and no. I always try to save as much as possible, but if you arrange dry food like pretzels next to wet food like watermelon, the dry food can be tough to salvage. If you present food in individual bowls, it can be saved if it's not

Follow the two-hour rule:
Perishable foods should be
thrown away after they've
been out for two hours.

perishable (think nuts, dried fruit, candy, or chips). If it is perishable (cheese, meat, etc.), you can hold onto it if it hasn't been out for more than two hours. Simply cover it with plastic wrap or beeswax wrap and refrigerate.

Food safety is important for produce too. It can be a little confusing to know whether you should wash fruits and veggies when you bring them home from the store or just before using them. For the most part, I wash my produce just before I use it. The internet is full of hacks to keep produce fresh, like wrapping them in paper towels or putting them in a vase, but honestly, why spend more time on food prep?

Berries and fresh herbs should be washed just before they are used, or else they can get moldy very quickly. When it's tray time, place them in a colander and rinse them well with cold running water. Drain them and blot them dry with paper towels or a clean kitchen towel. And you do not need to invest in a produce spray! Some foods, like radishes, require a little extra scrubbing to remove surface dirt, which can be done either with your hands or with a vegetable brush.

> Food safety is important for produce too.

And always, always wash your hands before prepping food, or anytime your hands come into contact with raw foods like eggs, meat, or poultry. And make sure kiddos and anyone else who is helping prepare or arrange food are doing the same.

5

KIDS AND SNACK TRAYS

MAKING TRAYS WITH—AND FOR—KIDDOS

There are perhaps no benefactors more excited about snack trays than kids—and the benefits of putting together trays for them go beyond how cool it is that they get to enjoy a whole tray of food. This is an incredible opportunity to give them some of their favorite snacks, introduce them to some new ones, and really balance the nutritional value of it all based on the stage of life they're in.

Getting Kids Involved

One of the things I love about school-age kids is how their brains light up when you give them a challenge. Kids love giving you their input! There have been many days when I've been stumped about what to add to an upcoming tray, but as soon as I ask my kids what to include, they flood me with ideas: "What about this, Mom?" "How about that?"

In addition to brainstorming ideas, kids can absolutely participate in putting snack trays together. As long as they have clean hands, kids as young as three or four can fill small bowls with fruit or dry snacks. Just be sure to have them handle foods they're allowed to eat (see "Trays for Ages and Stages" below). Kids ages four and up can help cut shapes out of fruit using cookie cutters. Just slice the fruit into slabs about half an inch thick, give them a cutting

One of the things I love about school-age kids is how their brains light up when you give them a challenge.

board and a demo of how to do it, and watch them work! You can buy cookie cutters with plastic handles, which can make the process easier for little hands.

Older kids and teens can put complete trays together by themselves. I remember how proud I felt when Willa presented a snack tray to her friends at a slumber party. She was able to display her independence, and her friends were super impressed. Sure, there weren't many fruits or veggies on the tray, but it was still a win in my book!

Trays for Ages and Stages

Snack trays are an excellent vehicle for including a variety of food in a kid's diet. In this section, we'll chat about some things to keep in mind when it comes to prepping snack trays for different age groups. But please don't take these suggestions as set rules or limitations. You know your kid best!

Babies and Toddlers

If you've had a baby or grandbaby in the past five years or so, you are probably familiar with baby-led weaning. It's a method of introducing solid foods to a baby by letting them feed themselves instead of being spoon-fed. It helps to develop oral motor skills and it's a wonderful thing to behold! It's also extremely messy. But feeding babies has never been a tidy endeavor.

The great thing about baby-led weaning is that babies who are ready for solids can partake along with the rest of the family in nearly every food. But of course, you want to serve foods in stage-appropriate shapes, sizes, and textures. And there are certain things to avoid.

Here are a few basics (based on recommendations from the American Academy of Pediatrics):

- Honey should never be given to infants under one year old.
- Cow's milk should not be offered until a child is one year old. Yogurt can be introduced at six months.

- Food pieces should either be bite-size or cut into stick shapes (about the length and width of a grown-up's pinkie) that a baby can gum or suck on. Round shapes shouldn't be given to babies, so make sure that items like grapes are cut into quarters (like I did for the Playdate Snacks on p. 146).
- Babies and toddlers should never be left alone while eating.
- Babies and toddlers should be encouraged to sit down while eating instead of running around or playing.
- Always provide a water cup when a baby or young child is eating.
- Popcorn is considered a choking hazard to kids under four.
- Other items that shouldn't be given to kids under four include hot dogs, chunks of meat or cheese, whole grapes, hard or sticky candy, chunks of nut butter, chunks of raw veggies, and chewing gum.

Elementary-Age Kids

Kids ages five and up are so adventurous and willing to learn, and they like to flex their skills in the kitchen. I remember when we had to do our Passover Seder via Zoom and Phoebe decided she was going to serve the matzah ball soup. She got up on a kitchen stool, grabbed the ladle, and started dishing out soup! I stood by to make sure she was OK, but she was perfectly capable of the task. I've talked to so many parents who say they want to cook more with their kids, but they hate the mess. Here's the truth: Cooking with kids will always be messier, but having them in the kitchen with you helps them learn so many vital lessons beyond using measuring cups. And there's only a window of time in which kids want to help in the kitchen, so grab it before it's gone! It's also a wonderful opportunity for busy parents to bond with their kids.

Here are some ideas for making trays with and for school-age kids:

- **Make them colorful!** Kids may not be *excited* about cauliflower, but I guarantee they'll be fascinated by the purple variety.

Cooking with kids will always
be messier, but it's a wonderful
opportunity for busy parents to
bond with their kids.

- **Let them pick.** Giving kids a say in their food choices can be a little tricky. Give them too many choices and they might never make up their minds. But it's fine to offer up to three choices when it comes to helping decide things like which snack tray to make together or what type of fruit to serve. Having a say helps kids feel invested in the food you prepare together, making them more likely to try it.

- **Be patient.** Even when kids take just a nibble or a sniff of a new food, that's still a positive step. It can take fifteen to twenty exposures to a new food for a child to even try it—let alone like it.

- **Always include protein.** Not only does protein help kids feel more satisfied with a snack, it's also vital for their growing bodies and will help ensure that they're not filling up only on crackers or chips. Keep in mind that protein is found not only in meat but also in cheese, nuts, nut butters, seeds, and beans.

Middle School–Age Kids

Not everything parenting experts say about middle school is true, but a fair share of it is. Middle school is often the first time kids start caring about their appearances and how other people perceive them. Unfortunately, it's also when stress about school and friends can mount and when eating disorders and disordered eating can develop. That's a scary thought, but it's even more reason for parents to keep talking about food and the importance of nourishing ourselves.

Here are some ideas for making trays with and for middle school kids:

- **Put them in charge.** While they might not be doing the grocery shopping yet, kids ages eleven to fourteen can certainly put a shopping list together! Ask them to choose a recipe from this book or online and create a shopping list based on that.

- **Make homemade chips.** Middle schoolers love their chips! There's no need to avoid potato chips, but you can also have fun by making your own veggie chips. Just thinly slice root veggies, like sweet potatoes, rutabaga, and beets, drizzle with olive oil, sprinkle with salt, and bake at 300°F for 30 to 40 minutes, until crisp.

- **Make pizza.** Kids of all ages love pizza, but middle schoolers will be more willing to experiment with toppings. Buy a store-bought crust or fresh pizza dough and let your kid pick out the toppings. This is a fun activity for a small party or sleepover. Don't forget to include the kids in the cleanup!

High School–Age Kids

If your teens are still willing to spend time in the kitchen with you, bravo! This means you've done a fabulous job of laying the groundwork when it comes to a healthy relationship with both your child and cooking. But these kids are busy, so you have to keep them engaged with interesting projects that make use of their autonomy.

Here are some ideas for making trays with and for high school kids:

- **Pick a theme.** Depending on what school they attend and their interests, high schoolers might be focused on musical theater, chemistry, or the French Revolution. Ask your teen to pick something they're interested in and then do a food project centered around that. If it's French cuisine, perhaps a chocolate soufflé is in order. Or pickling might be a fun tie-in for chemistry.

- **Let them do the shopping.** While a typical sixteen-year-old may not want to be seen with you at the mall, they're probably OK with being at the farmer's market or grocery store with you. Hand them some cash and let them know they'll be preparing whatever they choose. Then see what they come up with! Kids these days are far more sophisticated about food than my generation was, and they'll be thrilled that you're trusting them to make some choices.

- **Invite their friends.** The idea of letting your child and their friends take over your kitchen might cause you to break out in a cold sweat, but just hear me out. As long as you set some rules regarding cleaning up the kitchen and what tools can and can't be used, seeing what they come up with can be quite impressive. Kick back, pour yourself a drink, and get ready to be delighted—or maybe surprised. The idea is that you're trusting them to use the skills you've taught them. It's a great test drive before the college years.

6

MY FOOD PHILOSOPHY

A HEALTHY RELATIONSHIP
WITH FOOD STARTS WITH YOU

You may look at the mouthwatering photos of treat-filled trays in this book and wonder why a nutritionist would create a book that encourages so many foods that aren't exactly "nutritious." Great question! For too long, health professionals like me have gone around talking about "bad" and "good" foods. Certain foods, like those that are processed, have become demonized, and "clean" foods, like fresh fruits and veggies and certain proteins, have been put on a pedestal.

While I'm definitely in the business of trying to get folks to eat more fruits and veggies, it turns out that making people (including kids) feel bad about their less-than-perfect food choices doesn't actually lead them to eat healthier. What it can often do is backfire and cause people to eat in a disordered way, like bingeing on "bad" foods in secret or restricting what they eat during the week and then going wild on those "off-limits" foods during the weekend.

The goal in establishing a healthy, lifelong relationship with food is to be able to eat when you're hungry, stop when you're full, and include all types of foods in your diet. Food shouldn't make us feel bad or guilty, and obsessive thoughts about it shouldn't fill our days. It's there to sustain us, nourish us, help us grow and repair—and yes, celebrate moments in life, the big or the everyday.

With the impact of social media it might not feel like it, but you are the biggest influence on your kids and their feelings about food. That's why, starting from the very beginning of your child's life, it's vital for us as parents to model healthy behaviors, like eating our veggies and ditching the diet talk. When we have a good relationship with food and take an "everything can fit" approach instead of an all-or-nothing attitude, our kids will be more likely to do the same.

While achieving true balance in what we eat can be challenging, I strongly believe that exposing kids to all foods without judgment is the healthiest approach. That's why when I serve a snack tray to my family, I don't make my kids or hubby eat the baby carrots before the jelly beans. I don't want them to feel like they need to hide how much they're eating of any one food. I want to foster in my kids a healthy relationship with food that lasts well beyond their time in my house. If I've done that, I can feel great as a nutritionist and amazing as a parent.

> Food is there to sustain us, nourish us, help us grow and repair—and yes, celebrate moments in life, the big or the everyday.

That said, I do look for better-for-you options in candy and other treats. I always opt for items that are made with less sugar or that include whole grains—as long as they taste good. You do what's right for you. For the recipes featured on my trays, I follow the same guidelines, incorporating whole wheat flour and cutting back on added sweeteners but keeping the flavor of the product front and center. I encourage you to experiment and include as much variety on your trays as possible.

Ready to get on board? Let's go!

winter

The Magical Season 42

Time to Cozy Up 52

Is It Still Winter? 60

THE MAGICAL SEASON

Ah, the holidays! I'm pretty sure that the holiday season, which for us starts at American Thanksgiving and runs through New Year's Day, was created to get us through those incredibly dark, incredibly cold days of winter. At least in New York. Unless we light candles and fairy lights, put up whimsical decorations, and eat festive foods, how else would that time pass? Love them or hate them, I believe we need the holidays to survive winter (at least I know I do).

My mother, who emigrated from Germany after marrying my Brooklyn-born dad, was an amazing baker. She grew up in her parents' inn in Bad Nauheim, Germany. It was one of those classic Bavarian-style inns where you could order spaetzle and bratwurst and stay for a few nights as well. Thanks to her upbringing, we kids were the only ones in our small town who had tasted delicacies like red cabbage and apfelstrudel. And while Mom converted to Judaism when she married my father, the woman never stopped loving Christmas.

Around the holidays you'd find my mother sitting at the kitchen table, making dozens of vanillekipferl, almond crescent cookies bathed in a thick coating of powdered sugar.

While Mom didn't grow up Jewish, she made the most delicious, crispy latkes. I remember her telling me that absolutely under no circumstances could you add flour to the mixture—that was cheating—only hand-grated potatoes (the food processor makes them mushy), onion, an egg, and salt and pepper. And of course, lots and lots of oil to commemorate the miracle of the oil that burned in the temple of Jerusalem for eight nights instead of just one. Even if latkes aren't part of your usual holiday celebrations, I encourage you to try making them (see recipe on p. 46)! They're incredibly fun to serve on a snack tray with lots of extra toppings.

My kiddos are getting older, but even my teenager still gets excited about presents. While we normally open them in the evening during Chanukah, I always save a few small things to put in their holiday stockings. I know we're not the only Jewish family out there who adds a little Christmas flair into their celebration. I think it comes from growing up as practically the only Jewish kid in town and feeling so left out of the festivities. I begged my mom to get a Christmas tree for years. She finally relented and bought us a faux, snow-covered tree. I loved that thing, but it never failed to shed "snow" and glitter all over the floor, which we would have to vacuum up well into the spring.

Jon and the kids and I have been getting a holiday tree since we moved to the suburbs, and decorating it is something Jon does with the kids. And yes, we hang up those holiday stockings by the fireplace, and you better believe that Latke, our miniature long-haired dachshund, has his own personalized one too. I fill the stockings with small gifts the night before Christmas. In the morning we have a leisurely start to the day and enjoy a celebratory feast before opening gifts. Our Holiday Morning Platter has tree-shaped waffles (Leo's fave), Peppermint Whipped Cream (p. 48; great in coffee!), fresh berries, and turkey bacon, but I encourage you to make one that celebrates your own culture and heritage. Feel free to add any edible gifts you've received or holiday treats that are still kicking around the house.

> I encourage you to make a platter that celebrates your own culture and heritage.

Jon has never been big on going out for New Year's Eve, and since we've had kids in the mix for the last fourteen years, it's become a stay-at-home holiday for us. We get a fancy cake from our local bakery, and I make a fun party platter. The adults get champagne, and the kids get sparkling apple juice—fancy flutes for both. Then it's on to Twister and board games. I always stay up to watch the ball drop in Times Square, and now Willa joins me. No one else can keep their eyes open long enough. Not everyone loves ringing in the New Year, but I always look at it as another chance to chase your dreams.

Go as big on this tray as your imagination will take you! Besides my crowd-pleasing ginger cookies, everything else on the tray can be picked up from a store. If you'd like to create the marbled blue icing, simply add a few drops of natural blue food dye to royal icing (don't stir!), drag a toothpick through it, dip the tops of your cooled cookies into the icing, and let dry.

- Ginger Molasses Cookies (featured recipe)
- Candy canes
- Sugar cookies (store-bought or slice-and-bake)
- Fudge
- Peppermint bark
- Mandarin oranges
- Toffee chunks

Ginger Molasses Cookies

Makes about 3 dozen cookies.

The warm spices in these cookies will fill your home with such a cozy aroma. And if you're looking for that cookie that has the perfect amount of softness, this is it.

FOR DOUGH:
1 cup plus 2 tablespoons whole wheat flour
1 cup all-purpose flour
1½ teaspoons baking soda
¼ teaspoon salt
2 teaspoons ground ginger
¾ teaspoon ground cinnamon
½ teaspoon ground nutmeg
¼ teaspoon ground cardamom
½ cup (1 stick) unsalted butter, softened
¾ cup sugar
1 large egg, beaten
⅓ cup unsulfured molasses
1¼ teaspoons vanilla extract
⅔ cup chopped crystallized ginger

FOR ROLLING:
½ cup sugar
¼ teaspoon ground ginger
⅛ teaspoon ground cardamom

1 In a large bowl, whisk the flours, baking soda, salt, ground ginger, cinnamon, nutmeg, and cardamom.

2 In a separate bowl, cream the butter with the sugar using an electric hand mixer or stand mixer at medium speed. Beat in the egg. Add the molasses and vanilla and beat until incorporated. Reduce mixer speed to low and add the flour mixture in two to three additions until just incorporated. Stir in the crystallized ginger with a spatula. The dough should be very soft.

3 Form the dough into a ball and cover tightly with plastic wrap. Refrigerate 30 to 60 minutes or until firm enough to handle.

4 Preheat oven to 375°F. Line two baking sheets with parchment paper or silicone baking mats. In a small bowl, combine the sugar, ginger, and cardamom for rolling.

5 With your hands, roll the dough into 1-inch balls, then gently roll those in the sugar mixture. Place 3 inches apart on the baking sheets.

6 Bake 12 to 13 minutes, until the tops crack and the cookies are set. Transfer to a wire cooling rack and cool completely. Store in an airtight container up to a week.

LATKE TRAY

Traditional latke accompaniments are applesauce and sour cream. But why not broaden your horizons? As potato pancakes, latkes lend themselves to both savory and sweet toppings. It's fun to layer toppings too, such as lox, dill, red onion, and more.

- Traditional Potato Latkes (featured recipe)
- Sour cream or crème fraîche
- Lox
- Fresh dill
- Applesauce
- Beet hummus
- Red onion slices
- Lemon slices
- Cucumber slices
- Capers
- Spicy ketchup

Traditional Potato Latkes

Makes 8 latkes.

If you've never made latkes, the first thing you should know is that making them is a labor of love. While it's not complicated, there's a lot of hands-on work to make a delicious, crispy potato pancake. But they're SO worth it! My mom was big on hand-grating the potatoes and the onion. Sure, you could put them in a food processor—but when you do, the texture isn't the same and they tend to become dense when cooked, not light and crisp.

Note: If you have sensitive eyes when you're chopping onions, place the onion in the refrigerator or freezer for 15 to 20 minutes before handling.

1 pound Idaho potatoes, peeled
½ of a yellow onion
1 large egg, beaten
¼ teaspoon salt
¼ teaspoon pepper
½ cup olive oil

1 Using a box grater, coarsely grate the potatoes into a large bowl.

2 Transfer the shredded potatoes into a fine mesh sieve, place the sieve over a bowl, and press the potatoes with a wooden spoon, squeezing the excess water into the bowl. Discard the liquid and transfer the potatoes back to the original bowl.

3 Using a separate bowl, grate the onion and squeeze out the excess water like you did with the potatoes, then transfer the onions to the bowl with the potatoes. Add the egg, salt, and pepper, and combine.

4 Heat the oil in a large skillet over high heat until the oil is shimmering. Place a piece of grated potato in the pan. If it sizzles, you're ready to fry! Working in batches, add the potato mixture ¼ cup at a time to the pan, squeezing out any remaining liquid first. Flatten the tops of the latkes slightly with a spatula. Reduce heat to medium and cook about 5 minutes, until latkes are golden. Flip, and cook an additional 4 minutes.

5 Drain the latkes on a paper towel–lined plate. Latkes can be made a few hours in advance and reheated in a 200°F oven for 10 minutes. Arrange on a tray with accompaniments and serve.

HOLIDAY MORNING PLATTER

It's tough to rein in the enthusiasm on a holiday morning, and that often means that breakfast gets delayed until all the presents are opened. But since I like to nosh while the festivities are going on, I have this holiday platter ready to go before I hear those footsteps come running down the stairs. The Jacquet brand of tree-shaped waffles are fabulous, but if you can't find those, you can use a tree-shaped cookie cutter to create trees from frozen and toasted waffles. We used a mini waffle maker with a tree pattern to make the ones shown here. And don't forget to give everything a generous dusting of "snow" (aka powdered sugar) before serving.

- Peppermint Whipped Cream (featured recipe)
- Turkey bacon
- Frozen or premade waffles (tree-shaped if you can!)
- Frozen mini pancakes

- Raspberries
- Pomegranate seeds
- Chocolate-hazelnut spread
- Holiday jam
- Maple syrup

Peppermint Whipped Cream

Makes about 1½ cups.

So simple, but SO amazing! Homemade whipped cream is essential when you want to level up your holiday breakfast. And once you've made it, you'll wonder why you ever bought the stuff in the can.

1 cup heavy cream, very cold
¼ cup powdered sugar
⅛ teaspoon peppermint extract
1 tablespoon crushed peppermint candy, optional

1 Pour the cream in a medium bowl, preferably metal. Using a hand mixer or a stand mixer with a whisk attachment, beat on high 2 to 3 minutes, until stiff peaks start to form.

2 Add the powdered sugar and the extract and beat an additional minute.

3 Top with crushed peppermint candy just before serving. The whipped cream can be made one day in advance, covered, and refrigerated.

NEW YEAR'S EVE PARTY PLATTER

Even if you're staying home for New Year's, that doesn't mean you can't put on your LBD and heels! A little glam goes with this elegant but easy black-and-white tray. Make the cheese twists a day ahead so all you'll have to do is arrange everything on a board and pop open a bottle of your favorite bubbly.

- Black Sesame Parmesan Twists (featured recipe)
- Blackberries
- Chocolate sandwich cookies (such as Oreos)
- Chocolate wafer cookies (such as Loacker)
- Black-and-white cookies
- Chocolate-drizzled popcorn
- Fresh or dried black figs
- Black olive and baby mozzarella mini skewers
- Vanilla meringues
- Black licorice
- Crostini with plain goat cheese and fig-cocoa jam (such as Dalmatia)
- Black-and-white bow-tie pasta (such as Borgo de' Medici)

Black Sesame Parmesan Twists

Makes 20 twists.

So elegant and impressive but so doable, these twists are really fun to make. If you and your crew don't do sesame seeds, you can simply make them with Parmesan cheese. If you'd like to have your kiddos help with this one, bring them in to do the twisting after you've sliced the pastry into strips.

1 sheet puff pastry, thawed
1 tablespoon extra-virgin olive oil
⅛ teaspoon salt
2 tablespoons black sesame seeds
¼ cup grated Parmesan cheese

1 Preheat oven to 400°F. Line a baking sheet with parchment paper; set aside.

2 Unfold pastry sheet on a lightly floured surface. Using a rolling pin, lightly roll into a 10 × 14-inch rectangle.

3 Brush the entire surface of the pastry with oil. Sprinkle half with salt, sesame seeds, and Parmesan, and fold over. Gently press to seal.

4 Roll pastry lightly again until the rectangle is about 7 × 13 inches.

5 Using a pizza cutter, slice into about 26 (half-inch) strips. Twist and place on prepared baking sheet. Bake 10 minutes, or until golden. Twists can be stored in an airtight container at room temperature for three to four days.

TIME TO COZY UP

The winters are *long* in New York State. Some weekends are spent entirely indoors, which means I'm in the kitchen cooking, my husband is by the fireplace with the dog, Leo is playing *Just Dance*, and the girls are reading or using various electronics around the house.

If you are a parent, you understand that the meaning of Valentine's Day changes drastically once you have kids. While you and your partner may have gone out for a special, romantic Valentine's dinner during your courtship, those evenings pretty much evaporate post-kids. And the presents you both put lots of time and effort into finding might disappear too. But that's OK because they're replaced with a different type of Valentine's celebration with less Cupid and more *Frozen* and *Bluey*. The one thing that doesn't change? Chocolate. And lots of it!

While fresh strawberries are festive on their own, a layer or two of chocolate never hurts. And whether you're more into candy hearts or chocolate samplers, there's always room on the tray for Chocolate-Dipped Strawberries (p. 54), which my kids love to help me make.

Occasionally we get a really big dump of snow, and the kids and I walk down to the local park to go sledding. Once we get home, peel back the snow-packed snowsuits, and remove all the damp layers, it's time to warm up.

I fell in love with hot chocolate when my mom brought me to Amsterdam on one of our trips to Europe. We stayed at a small bed-and-breakfast that provided a continental breakfast. I remember asking my mom what *continental* meant. She explained that it was the opposite of an "American" breakfast and just included the basics, like toast, jam, a soft-boiled egg, juice, coffee, or in my case, hot chocolate.

But this Nederlanden hot chocolate wasn't cocoa from a packet, and it was like nothing I'd ever had before. It wasn't watery in the least. It was so incredibly rich, in fact, that I had to use a spoon to drink it. I have been trying to re-create it for the past forty years! My kids love to try my variations, but the main thing they love about hot chocolate is all the toppings—whipped cream, marshmallows, and sprinkles. They want it all!

The Hot Cocoa Mix recipe (p. 56) that's featured on the Hot Chocolate Bar is so delicious and easy to make that I highly recommend gifting it to friends and family. You can put it in a decorative jar and tie a festive ribbon around the top. I like to attach a little recipe tag that explains how to make a cup.

Even though I no longer love cold weather as much as I used to, I do enjoy the occasional snow day. Especially when I've been smart enough to stock up on the essentials and we've got plenty of wood for the fireplace. There's something relaxing about knowing that you don't have to rush through breakfast to get to the bus stop on time or pick anyone up from school. Movies can be started in the middle of the day—unless of course folks are still busy sledding. Snow days are also an excellent excuse to make something hearty and savory, like chili with all the fixings. If you've never done a chili night, it's a fun way to enjoy that classic winter warmer. And the Snow Day Tray is excellent for capping off a snowy day with friends, if you can shovel a path between your house and your neighbors'.

> The main thing my kids love about hot chocolate is all the toppings— whipped cream, marshmallows, and sprinkles. They want it all!

VALENTINE'S DAY TRAY

From chocolates to gummy candy, there is never a dearth of heart-shaped sweets around Valentine's Day. I like to balance out all the packaged stuff with some hand-dipped chocolate strawberries. And Brie is perfect for anyone who claims they don't have a sweet tooth.

- Chocolate-Dipped Strawberries (featured recipe)
- Valentine's Day mini cupcakes
- Heart-shaped chocolates
- Pink or red M&M's
- Lollipops
- Heart- or kiss-shaped fruit gummies
- Heart-shaped Brie (If you can't find this shape in your store's cheese section, simply transform a regular wheel of Brie using a large heart-shaped cookie cutter.)
- Heart-shaped brownies (Make a batch from a box and cut out hearts.)
- Fresh cherries (If you can't find fresh ones, get frozen cherries and defrost them.)
- Blood orange slices

Chocolate-Dipped Strawberries

Makes about 25 medium or 12 large berries.

12 ounces fresh strawberries
1 cup semisweet chocolate chips
½ cup white chocolate chips

When you're using so few ingredients, you want to make sure you choose the best ones. Look for strawberries with extra-long stems, which make them easier for dipping and are available around Valentine's Day. And opt for high-quality chocolate chips.

1 Place berries in a colander and rinse well. Drain and blot completely dry with paper towels.

2 Line a baking sheet with parchment paper; set aside.

3 Place semisweet chocolate chips in a microwave-safe bowl and heat for 1 minute. Stir with a spatula. If the chocolate needs more time to melt, heat for an additional 30 seconds and stir again.

4 Dip berries into chocolate and place on prepared baking sheet. If the chocolate in the bowl begins to harden during the dipping process, put it back in the microwave for 30 seconds. Place the baking sheet in the refrigerator for 20 minutes or until chocolate is firm.

5 Place white chocolate chips in a microwave-safe bowl and heat for 1 minute. Stir with a spatula. Set aside half of the chocolate-covered berries. Dip the remaining half of the strawberries in the white chocolate. Place the berries back on the baking sheet and refrigerate for another 15 to 20 minutes, until set. Enjoy!

HOT CHOCOLATE BAR

The only thing better than warming up with a frothy mug of hot cocoa is dressing it up with all the toppings on this fabulous bar. If you don't have time to make the hot cocoa mix, you have my permission to use one from the store. Look for fair-trade cocoa mixes, which ensure that cocoa farmers receive a fair wage for their cocoa beans.

- Hot Cocoa Mix (featured recipe)
- Whipped cream
- Sprinkles
- Chocolate bar pieces
- Chocolate chip cookies
- Hot cocoa bombs (You can find these at Target or Williams-Sonoma.)
- Mini muffins

- Mini marshmallows
- Cinnamon sticks or ground cinnamon
- Long vanilla wafer cookies (such as Loacker)
- White chocolate chips
- Mint M&M's
- Andes candies
- Peppermint sticks

Hot Cocoa Mix

Makes 20 servings.

You may be tempted to skip the sifting step, but it's key to keeping your cocoa mix from clumping. It does take a few minutes longer, but the result will be so much better. This is a wonderful homemade treat to give as a gift to family or bring as a hostess gift to a gathering. Add a ribbon to the jar, along with a tag with instructions for making a mug.

1 cup unsweetened cocoa powder (such as
  Equal Exchange)
1½ cups sugar
1 teaspoon salt
1 cup mini marshmallows, optional

1 Using a fine-mesh sieve, sift the cocoa powder into a large bowl. Add the sugar and salt to the bowl and use a whisk to combine.

2 Carefully transfer the cocoa mixture to a large (about 20-ounce) lidded glass jar. Top with the marshmallows if desired. Seal the jar until ready to use.

To make hot cocoa: Warm 1 cup of milk (I use whole or oat milk) in the microwave and stir in 2 tablespoons of the mix. If you're making more than one serving, heat the milk on the stove in a small saucepan until hot but not boiling, and whisk in the cocoa.

SNOW DAY TRAY

On those below-freezing days, I can't think of anything more satisfying than a steaming bowl of chili. This tray has a lot of elements, but you can gather them quickly by asking your crew to help pull them out of the fridge and pantry and transfer them to small bowls. And if you're out of something, tell your neighbor you'll trade them a bowl of chili for it.

- Bison and Black Bean Chili (featured recipe)
- Corn bread muffins or mini loaves
- Hot honey (such as Mike's)
- Unsalted butter
- Diced avocado
- Shredded cheddar cheese
- Cilantro
- Chopped scallions
- Sliced radishes
- Sour cream or crème fraîche
- Tortilla chips
- Saltines or oyster crackers
- Brown rice (Use the 90-second microwavable packets, such as Ready Rice.)
- Bacon bits
- Guacamole
- Crumbled queso fresco

Bison and Black Bean Chili

Makes 8 servings.

This chili is the perfect balance between spicy and earthy. It has enough flavor for the grown-ups but not so much that it will overwhelm the kids. It comes together quickly and can be kept warm in a slow cooker when it's ready to serve. You can substitute ground beef or turkey for the bison if desired. This chili is equally delicious and hearty without the meat!

2 tablespoons olive oil
1 small onion, peeled and finely chopped
2 teaspoons ground cumin
1 teaspoon chili powder
1 teaspoon ground cinnamon
1 tablespoon unsweetened cocoa powder
½ teaspoon sea salt
½ teaspoon freshly ground black pepper
1 pound ground bison, ground beef, or ground turkey
½ cup shredded carrots

1 (15-ounce) can black beans, rinsed and drained
2 cups low-sodium chicken broth
1 (28-ounce) can crushed tomatoes
1 orange or red bell pepper, seeded and diced

1 Heat the oil in a large stockpot over medium heat. Add the onion and sauté until soft, about 2 minutes. Add the cumin, chili powder, cinnamon, cocoa powder, salt, and pepper, and stir. Add the meat and cook 5 minutes, breaking up with a spatula. Add the carrots, beans, broth, tomatoes, and bell pepper and bring to a boil. Reduce heat, cover, and simmer 20 minutes. Taste and adjust seasonings to your preference.

2 Spoon chili into bowls, add toppings, and enjoy! Leftover chili can be stored for three to four days in an airtight container or frozen for up to three months.

IS IT STILL WINTER?

Please don't tell Willa, but March—her birthday month—is my least favorite month of the year. When I was a magazine editor, I always struggled to come up with recipe ideas for that month. People are sick of soups and stews by that point, but salads and lighter fare aren't quite right either. The fallback for the food section of the magazine was often "Pizza Night!" or "New Pasta Ideas!" which were the best ways to deal with that in-between time.

While you might be wishing for backyard barbecues and picnics by this time of year, most of the country is still in a deep freeze. But of course, there's always *something* to celebrate. Like an excellent report card, a high-scoring basketball game, or a much-improved test score. Or really anything! When it feels like everyone just needs a midweek dose of sunshine, I make a batch of my Peanut Butter Blossom Cookies (p. 62). These go well with anything you have on hand, like apple slices, cheddar cheese, crackers, or carrots—whatever you and your kiddos like.

One way to make an easy snack tray that feels over-the-top in the best possible way is to take one ingredient and just own it. Do *all* the things with that one ingredient. This is both fun and unfussy. If you love cheese, do everything cheese, from crackers to bread to fondue. Since my whole family loves peanut butter, we go all in on a Peanut Butter Everything Tray. Fortunately, peanut butter is a versatile ingredient, lending itself not only to sweet but also to savory applications.

> There's always *something* to celebrate.

I definitely gravitate toward things that are small and cute, like our mini long-haired dachshund, Latke. And while large-scale trays look impressive, going mini can be very fun. When it's time for something a little different, I grab my smallest canning jars and make

Jarcuterie, which is just a charming word for charcuterie in a jar. These are such a delight to create, so I love getting the whole crew involved in making them. They can really let their imaginations run wild with these—veggies, fruit, cheese, meat, and crackers are all fair game. And it's fun to add a skewer or two that's loaded up with olives, cherry tomatoes, cornichons (aka baby pickles), and baby bocconcini. You can even add a layer of roasted nuts or seasoned beans on the bottom of your jars. Your jar is your oyster!

AWESOME REPORT CARD PLATTER

Some kids get amazing grades all the time; others not so much. That's why it's nice to offer up a little celebration when your child puts in the extra work to improve their grades. The items on this tray are just suggestions. Choose whatever would make your kiddo's day and get ready to cheer with a glass of milk.

- Peanut Butter Blossom Cookies (featured recipe)
- Two-bite brownies
- Strawberries
- Snap-pea crisps
- Peanut butter filled pretzels
- White cheddar cheese
- Crackers (such as Triscuit)
- Cherry tomatoes
- Carrots
- Favorite dressing for dipping

Peanut Butter Blossom Cookies

Makes 15 cookies.

Since these classic holiday cookies are SO good (and they're the only cookie Phoebe likes), I make them year-round. You can make these vegan by swapping the regular butter for plant butter and opting for an egg replacer. Agave syrup can replace the honey as well. I haven't found the perfect replacement for the Hershey's Kisses, but you can use a large chocolate chip in the center instead. I like the combination of all-purpose and whole wheat flour because it provides the right amount of tenderness while also adding whole grain goodness.

½ cup (1 stick) unsalted butter, softened
½ cup creamy natural peanut butter
½ cup packed brown sugar
2 tablespoons honey
1 large egg, beaten
1 teaspoon vanilla extract
1 cup all-purpose flour
¾ cup whole wheat flour
1 teaspoon baking soda
¼ teaspoon sea salt
½ cup sugar for rolling
15 Hershey's Kisses, unwrapped

1 Preheat oven to 375°F. Line a baking sheet with parchment paper or a silicone baking mat.

2 Using a hand mixer, cream the butter in a medium bowl. Add the peanut butter, brown sugar, honey, egg, and vanilla, and mix again on medium.

3 In a separate bowl, combine the flours, baking soda, and salt. Add the wet ingredients to the dry and combine. Form the dough into a ball, wrap in plastic wrap, and chill for about 20 minutes, until firm.

4 Place the sugar in a small bowl; set aside. Use an ice cream scoop to scoop about 1 tablespoon of dough at a time. Roll the dough into balls and then gently roll the balls of dough in the sugar. Place on the baking sheet about 2 inches apart.

5 Bake 9 to 10 minutes, until the tops of the cookies are cracked. Remove from oven and press Kisses (or chocolate chips) into the centers of the cookies. Allow to cool slightly and enjoy.

PEANUT BUTTER EVERYTHING TRAY

I acknowledge that not everyone is a peanut butter fan, but you can make a similar tray with another nut or seed butter—like almond, cashew, or even pistachio butter. And for folks who are allergic to peanuts, you can use sunflower seed butter to make the grilled cheese and ants on a log, and it's fairly easy to find sunflower-butter-filled pretzels and chocolate cups these days.

- PB Grilled Cheese (featured recipe)
- Apple slices
- Frozen chocolate-covered banana bites (such as Diana's)
- Strawberries

- Peanuts
- Peanut-butter-dipped banana bites (such as Barnana)
- Peanut butter M&M's
- Ants on a log (celery, peanut butter, and raisins)

- Peanut butter
- Peanut-butter-filled pretzels
- Peanut butter cups (such as Justin's)

PB Grilled Cheese

Makes 1 sandwich.

OK, let me explain. It's true that while we often pair everyone's favorite creamy spread with sweet things like jelly, peanut butter can also play well with savory ingredients like cheese. I love how the cheese combines with the creamy peanut butter to make a sensational sammie, but it may not be your jam (see what I did there?). Still, if you're a PB lover, I recommend giving it a try.

2 teaspoons unsalted butter, room temperature
2 slices sourdough or other bread of choice
Cooking spray
⅓ cup shredded sharp cheddar cheese
   (Use hand-shredded cheese from a block for better melting.)
2 tablespoons creamy peanut butter

1 Spread 1 teaspoon of butter onto one side of each bread slice.

2 Spray a large skillet or griddle with cooking spray, and heat on medium-high. Place one slice of bread in the pan, butter side down, for 1 minute.

3 Evenly top the bread in the pan with the cheese, and cook for an additional minute, until the cheese melts.

4 Spread the peanut butter on the unbuttered side of the remaining slice of bread. Place the bread peanut butter side down on top of the cheese-topped bread in the pan. Flip sandwich and cook 1 more minute.

5 Remove sandwich from the pan with a spatula, place it on a cutting board, and let it sit for 1 minute. Slice in half and serve.

JARCUTERIE

These might seem a little fussy, but they are seriously fun to make! Once again, there are no rules to this! But it's nice to vary your ingredients and make some jars that have only veggies, grapes, and olives for anyone who doesn't eat animal products. Older kids who can handle the skewers (around seven and up) can help assemble these. Make combinations that you enjoy. Phoebe loves cornichons, so her skewers always have several. You can even add little signs with guests' names on them. Grown-ups may want to pair their jars with a glass of rosé. Just a thought!

- Quick Pickled Cucumbers and Radishes (featured recipe)
- Marinated Baby Bocconcini (see bonus recipe, or substitute mozzarella pearls)
- Pitted olives
- Manchego cheese (or another hard cheese, like Parmesan or aged gouda), cut into triangles
- Jarred marinated peppers (such as Peppadew)
- Grapes
- Berries

- Salami slices
- Pepperoncini
- Flatbread crackers
- Nuts
- Dried apricots
- Cornichons
- Nut and fruit crackers (such as Raincoast Crisps)
- 6- to 8-inch wooden skewers and small jars or glasses

Quick Pickled Cucumbers and Radishes

If you haven't made quick pickles before, get ready to impress yourself. You will be amazed by how easy they are to make and how delicious they are. My kids gobble them up for days. If you don't like radishes, simply add another cucumber or two.

¾ cup white vinegar
1 teaspoon salt
1 teaspoon sugar
4 Kirby cucumbers, cut lengthwise into quarters
2 watermelon radishes, sliced
1 clove garlic, sliced
¼ cup chopped fresh dill
1 dried bay leaf

1 Combine the vinegar, salt, and sugar in a medium saucepan and bring to a simmer. Whisk and remove from heat.

2 Meanwhile, place the cucumbers, radishes, garlic, dill, and bay leaf in a heat-safe bowl.

3 Carefully pour the hot pickling liquid over the vegetables and stir. Cover and chill for about 1 hour, or until cold. You can remove the vegetables and reuse the pickling liquid to make another batch.

Marinated Baby Bocconcini

You can usually find marinated bocconcini, but not always, so I wanted to come up with my own recipe for making it. You can keep this in the refrigerator for up to a week. Use any remaining bocconcini in salads, on pizza, or tossed with pasta.

1 (7-ounce) container of baby bocconcini (fresh mozzarella pearls)
¼ cup extra-virgin olive oil
⅛ teaspoon salt
¼ teaspoon pepper
¼ teaspoon dried thyme
¼ teaspoon dried basil
⅛ teaspoon crushed red pepper

1 Drain the bocconcini in a colander. Don't throw out the container!

2 Place bocconcini back in the container and add the remaining ingredients, tossing to coat. Marinate in the refrigerator for 20 minutes or more before adding to jarcuterie.

spring

Celebrating the Season 72

Come Out and Play 90

CELEBRATING THE SEASON

The days might still be gray, but once St. Patrick's Day arrives, you know spring is just around the corner. And while I don't have one drop of Irish blood in my family tree, I always feel like it's appropriate to celebrate St. Patrick, the patron saint of Ireland, and everything green and springy.

My St. Paddy's Day tray includes lots of traditional Irish foods, like soda bread, cabbage, cheddar, and corned beef, as well as store-bought cupcakes and cookies—plus a mini version of everyone's favorite green shake but with less sugar (p. 74). And since it's mini, it's the perfect size for everyone to enjoy.

Whether or not your family celebrates any of the spring religious holidays, the season provides endless reasons to look forward to a fresh, new, joyful season. I am not an expert gardener, but I love to get out in the yard and get our planters and garden beds ready for new plantings come spring. My kids don't love it, but I incentivize them to help by letting them pick out plants at the garden center, and then I thank them for participating with a spring-themed snack tray.

Your kid might insist that they hate carrots, but I'm pretty sure you'll be able to convert them to being carrot fans with the Carrot Cake Muffins with Cream Cheese Frosting (p. 76) that are the centerpiece of the Spring Fling Snacks. You can serve them with strawberries, spring-themed chocolates, pistachios, jelly beans, deviled eggs, and anything else that's colorful and springy.

It can be a bummer to stay home for spring break when your besties are on tropical vacations. Willa always loves to tell me that she's the only one in her friend group who hasn't traveled internationally. I mean, the deprivation! But if you can't get away, why not bring the vacay vibes to your home? The Staycation Snack Tray is definitely one of my favorites to create. It's whimsical, it's colorful, and it features Tropical Fruit and Yogurt Parfaits (p. 80), which include many of my most-loved ingredients, like mango and dragon fruit.

Once May finally makes her arrival, I feel like I can relax a little and start to spread my wings a bit. I clean off the outdoor sofa and set up the cushions. The grill gets scrubbed and ready for the barbecues in our future. There's a sense of anticipation in the air for what's to come in the months ahead. And my kids start the countdown to the end of school. What better way to usher in May than with a Cinco de Mayo celebration? Individual five-layer dips for the kids (p. 82) and margaritas for the adults (p. 98).

I'll be the first to admit that I expect to be pampered on Mother's Day. I don't need a day at the spa or anything fancy, but I do expect to get to sleep in, enjoy breakfast in bed, and choose where to spend the day. Come on, it's the *one* day that moms get to be selfish, so please indulge us, thank you very much! If you happen to be the one making breakfast in bed, just know that Mom doesn't necessarily need a ginormous tray—just one with all her favorites. For me that means a really good, hot cup of coffee, a croissant, a well-cooked egg, fruit salad, and excellent chocolate—oh, and homemade cards will always win my heart. Kids may need a little supervision putting this tray together and delivering it to mom, but they can certainly help assemble it. Phoebe loves to make fried eggs!

> There's a sense of anticipation in the air for what's to come in the months ahead.

If moms get their day, then dads should too. My biggest gift to Jon is basically just not asking him to do any household tasks on Father's Day. If he wants to go out for a two-hour bike ride followed by a one-hour cooldown/stretch, I will support that. Jon's not into grilling, so I'm happy to put on my apron, grab the tongs, and cook up some delicious hot dogs, complete with *all* the toppings, of course. And since I believe there should always be an equilibrium between plant and animal options, I balance those dogs out with my version of a three-bean salad (p. 88).

ST. PATRICK'S DAY SNACK TRAY

The whole point of this tray is for it to feel very springlike. So if there are other green foods you'd like to fill the platter with, go for it. But the Mint Cream Mini Shakes are a must and will bring out your inner leprechaun.

- Mint Cream Mini Shakes (featured recipe)
- Pistachios, shelled
- St. Patrick's Day cookies and/or mini cupcakes
- Cucumber spears
- Granny Smith apple slices
- Green M&M's

- Seaweed shamrocks
- Broccoli florets
- Soda bread, cut into slices
- Kale crackers (such as RW Garcia)
- Irish cheddar cheese
- Corned beef slices
- Sauerkraut

Mint Cream Mini Shakes

Makes 6 (¼ cup) servings. (Use 6 small glasses, such as shot glasses.)

Enjoying a minty, green shake is a much-anticipated rite of spring for many folks. I find some versions to be a bit over the top in terms of sweetness and flavor, but they're certainly fun! My version is a little bit healthier (no syrups or dyes) and a lot smaller but still delivers that creamy, minty payoff.

1 cup vanilla ice cream
½ cup milk of your choice
¼ teaspoon peppermint extract
A few drops natural green food coloring
½ cup whipped cream
Handful fresh mint, for garnish

1 Combine the ice cream, milk, extract, and food coloring in a blender. Blend on high until frothy.

2 Divide the shake among the small glasses. Top each with a dollop of whipped cream and a fresh mint leaf and serve.

SPRING FLING SNACKS

You may be able to find premade deviled eggs at your local store. If not, I've added a bonus recipe in this section that can be quickly whipped up using store-bought hard-boiled eggs.

- Carrot Cake Muffins with Cream Cheese Frosting (featured recipe)
- Fresh berries
- Mini chocolate eggs
- Pistachios, shelled

- Jelly beans
- Pastel-colored Jordan almonds
- Quick Deviled Eggs (see bonus recipe)
- Bunny-shaped chocolates

Carrot Cake Muffins

Makes 15 muffins.

Trust me on something—I tried using pre-shredded carrots, and that does *not* work. You really need to grate the carrots finely to get a tender and moist muffin. These make perfect after-school snacks or breakfast on the go. The cream cheese frosting is not too sweet, which is exactly how my kids like it.

Cooking spray
1½ cups all-purpose flour
½ cup whole wheat flour
¼ teaspoon salt
1 teaspoon baking powder
1 teaspoon baking soda
¾ cup brown sugar
1 teaspoon ground cinnamon
⅓ cup chopped walnuts, optional
1 teaspoon vanilla extract
Juice and zest of a lemon
2 large eggs, beaten
¾ cup extra-virgin olive oil or melted butter
2 cups shredded carrots (grate on smallest hole of box grater or use food processor)

1 Preheat oven to 350°F. Line a 12-cup muffin pan with liners. Spray liners with cooking spray and set aside.

2 In a medium bowl, combine the flours, salt, baking powder, baking soda, brown sugar, cinnamon, and walnuts.

3 In a separate bowl, combine the vanilla, lemon zest and juice, eggs, oil, and carrots. Add the wet ingredients to the dry and combine.

4 Fill muffin liners about three-fourths full, and bake 20 to 22 minutes, until tops are dry to the touch. Cool completely before frosting.

CREAM CHEESE FROSTING

12 ounces (1½ blocks) plain cream cheese, softened
1 cup powdered sugar
Pinch salt
1 teaspoon vanilla extract
1 teaspoon lemon zest

1 In a medium bowl, beat the cream cheese with the sugar until blended, about 2 minutes. Add the salt, vanilla, and zest, and beat another 30 seconds.

2 If the frosting is too soft, cover and refrigerate 20 to 30 minutes, until firmer. Transfer frosting to a disposable piping bag. Snip off the end and pipe frosting onto the tops of the muffins. You could also pipe a little orange and green frosting on top in the shape of carrots!

Quick Deviled Eggs

8 precooked and peeled hard-boiled eggs
3 tablespoons mayonnaise
2 tablespoons Dijon mustard
1 tablespoon fresh lemon juice
¼ teaspoon salt
¼ teaspoon black pepper
Finely chopped chives and/or dill for
   garnish

1 Slice the eggs in half and use a teaspoon to gently scoop the yolks into a medium bowl. Place the egg whites on a plate or platter.

2 Add the mayonnaise, mustard, lemon juice, salt, and pepper to the yolks and mash with a large fork until smooth. Using a small spoon, fill the egg whites with the deviled egg mixture. Serve immediately or refrigerate until ready to serve. Garnish just before serving.

STAYCATION SNACK TRAY

This is one of my favorite trays to put together! There is something so magical to me about vibrant tropical fruits. And these days you can find all these fruits in season (from somewhere in the world) year-round.

- Tropical Fruit and Yogurt Parfaits (featured recipe)
- Kiwifruit, golden or green
- Watermelon wedges
- Dragon fruit or papaya
- Mango
- Pineapple spears
- Dry-roasted macadamia nuts (such as Mauna Loa)

Tropical Fruit and Yogurt Parfaits

Makes 4 servings. (Use 4 dessert or parfait glasses.)

When I need to pretend that I'm in a warm, beautiful spot by the ocean, my thoughts always bring me back to the time I spent in Australia as a student. I was in my early twenties, single, and ready to travel pretty much anywhere. Luckily, I had a good friend with a VW Bus, and we hit all the beach towns on the northeastern coast, enjoying lots of fresh mangoes along the way. This yogurt parfait might not take the place of a tropical trip, but it delivers the vacay vibes.

¼ cup macadamia nuts
1 cup diced fresh mango (about 1 large mango)
2 cups vanilla whole-milk yogurt
1 cup diced fresh or frozen dragon fruit (about ½ a dragon fruit)
1 cup diced fresh pineapple
¼ cup coconut chips (such as Bare brand)
Dragon fruit chips (such as NOW Foods brand), optional

1 Preheat oven or toaster oven to 350°F.

2 Place nuts on a baking sheet and bake 5 minutes. Cool, chop, and set aside.

3 Place ¼ cup of the mango in the bottom of each of the dessert or parfait glasses.

4 Top the mango with ¼ cup yogurt and add ¼ cup dragon fruit.

5 Add another ¼ cup yogurt, then top with ¼ cup pineapple, 1 tablespoon coconut chips, and 1 tablespoon macadamia nuts. Garnish with a dragon fruit chip and head to the (pretend) tropics!

CINCO DE MAYO CELEBRATION

Since the fifth of May can land on any day of the week, I love how easy it is to put this tray together. The dip can be assembled a few hours in advance and refrigerated until ready to serve, and the quesadillas can be made in just minutes. And take a look in your grocery store's frozen section—you may be able to find some premade quesadillas there as well.

- Mini Five-Layer Dip (featured recipe)
- Tortilla chips, blue or regular
- Salsa
- Guacamole
- Lime wedges
- Radish slices
- Scallion slices
- Quesadillas (see bonus recipe)

Mini Five-Layer Dip

Makes 4 servings. (Use 4 small ramekins or glasses.)

These individual dips accomplish two things: First, they're super flavorful and fun. Second, they help prevent little (or big) hands from double-dipping. (When Leo was little, he was known to keep loading up his chips with more guac from the bowl.) They're perfect for a family-style Cinco de Mayo celebration or for a tailgate party.

1 ripe avocado, pitted
Zest and juice of 1 lime
¼ teaspoon salt, divided
¼ teaspoon black pepper, divided
1 (15-ounce) can black beans, drained and rinsed
¼ cup crème fraîche, sour cream, or plain Greek yogurt
½ cup salsa
1 scallion, sliced thinly

1 Place the avocado in a small bowl and smash with a fork. Add the lime zest and juice and half of the salt and pepper and combine.

2 Place the black beans in a separate bowl and mash with a fork until about half the beans are smashed. Stir in the remaining salt and pepper.

3 Spoon one-fourth of the avocado mixture followed by one-fourth of the black bean mixture into each of the ramekins or glasses. Add 1 tablespoon of the crème fraîche, sour cream, or yogurt, followed by 2 tablespoons of salsa to each. Top each with 1 teaspoon of the scallion and party!

Quesadillas

Cooking spray
3 (6-inch) corn tortillas
¾ cup Mexican blend shredded cheese

1 Spray a nonstick skillet with cooking spray and heat on medium-high. Add one tortilla to the pan.

2 Evenly place ¼ cup of the cheese on one half of the tortilla. Allow cheese to melt for 1 minute, then use a spatula to fold the tortilla in half. Heat for an additional minute, until the edges are golden. Repeat with the remaining tortillas and cheese. Slice quesadillas into wedges and serve.

MOTHER'S DAY BREAKFAST-IN-BED TRAY

Whether your kids are two or twelve, you're always doing something for them when you're a mom. While you should totally kick back and enjoy breakfast in bed, you—or another adult—will need to provide a little supervision while this tray is put together. And depending on how old your kiddos are, they may also need help delivering the tray.

- Minted Fruit Salad (featured recipe)
- Croissant
- Coffee
- Cream/milk
- Jam
- Fried egg (or however Mom likes her eggs)
- Chocolate truffles (The ones from Vosges are fabulous.)
- Butter
- Flowers

Minted Fruit Salad

Makes 8 servings.

I'm a fruit lover—I pretty much enjoy every fruit on the planet. Regular fruit salads are lovely, but for a special occasion, I like to make a little dressing to elevate the flavor of the combination of fruits. This salad is so refreshing and pretty and will definitely help make Mom's day. The fruit salad can be assembled the night before. Simply wait to add the mint dressing until just before serving.

1 peppermint tea bag
⅓ cup water
2 cups cubed watermelon
1 cup fresh raspberries
2 cups hulled and quartered strawberries
⅓ cup pomegranate seeds
1 cup green grapes, halved if large
1 teaspoon honey
1 tablespoon fresh mint leaves

1 Place the tea bag in a mug or heat-safe liquid-measuring cup. Boil the water, then pour it over the tea bag. Let it steep for 10 minutes.

2 Meanwhile, in a large bowl, gently combine the fruit with a spatula.

3 Remove the tea bag from the mug and stir the honey and mint into the tea. Drizzle over the fruit, chill for at least 10 minutes, and serve.

FATHER'S DAY BOARD

To assemble this tray, you'll want to have several ramekins for condiments and a separate tray for the cooked hot dogs and buns. The toppings may seem random, but they're not, and there's no need to offer all of them. Just pick the ones your family likes best and use those. They can be combined to make hot dogs in the following styles:

BANH MI: shredded carrots + mini cucumbers + spicy mayo
BALLPARK: onion + ketchup + yellow mustard
COBB: avocado + hard-boiled egg + bacon + chopped cabbage
BBQ: barbecue sauce + baked beans + pickle slices
MEXICAN: guacamole + Cotija cheese + cilantro + salsa verde

- Modern Three-Bean Salad (featured recipe)
- Hot dogs and buns
- Ketchup
- Yellow mustard
- Relish
- Chopped onion
- Baked beans
- Diced avocado
- Crumbled bacon
- Cilantro
- Sliced mini cucumbers
- Spicy mayo
- Shredded carrots
- Chopped cabbage or romaine lettuce
- Barbecue sauce
- Pickle slices
- Chopped, packaged hard-boiled eggs
- Cotija cheese, crumbled
- Salsa verde
- Guacamole

Modern Three-Bean Salad

Makes 6 servings.

I have always loved three-bean salad. During my vegetarian years, it was often the only thing I could eat at potlucks and barbecues. But the traditional recipes call for up to ⅓ cup of sugar, which really doesn't seem necessary for a salad. I still like a little bit of sweetness from the honey.

⅓ cup apple cider vinegar
3 tablespoons extra-virgin olive oil
1 tablespoon honey
½ teaspoon salt
¼ teaspoon black pepper

¼ cup red onion, finely chopped
1 (15-ounce) can black beans, drained and rinsed
1 (15-ounce) can cannellini beans, drained and rinsed
1 (15-ounce) can garbanzo beans, drained and rinsed
1 cup celery, chopped (about 3 to 4 stalks)
¼ cup chopped flat-leaf parsley

1 In a large bowl, whisk together the vinegar, oil, honey, salt, pepper, and onion. Add the beans, celery, and parsley, and combine with a spatula or wooden spoon.

2 Refrigerate until ready to serve.

COME OUT AND PLAY

Quick—what food says "springtime" to you? Is it berries? Burgers? Ice cream? Well, get ready, because you'll find all of them in this chapter, beginning with the unofficial start of American summer, Memorial Day! When I was a teenager, Memorial Day always meant a picnic with my friends at Allegany State Park. It wasn't warm enough to go for a swim in the lake, but the warm sun was plenty to get us excited about the season ahead. And I hope my Memorial Day Burger Tray conjures up similar feelings for you and your crew.

To be honest, we eat ice cream all year long, but our consumption of the creamy frozen treat does pick up in the warmer months. When you want to elevate your everyday bowl of vanilla, it's time for an Ice Cream Social Tray with homemade caramel sauce and all the other toppings you can dream up, from sprinkles to maraschino cherries to chunks of cookie dough—the sky is the limit!

When the weather starts heating up, my enthusiasm for cooking over a hot stove starts to dwindle. That's why it's nice to have easy recipes in your back pocket, like tacos. Tacos are probably my favorite family meal because literally *everyone* can assemble their favorite combination of ingredients, and even my picky eaters are satisfied. Of course, we always include seasoned black beans for Willa, and you can use my Adobo-Spiced Ground Turkey recipe (p. 96) with any ground meat, including plant-based substitutes.

We love having friends over, but the more I overthink and stress about cleaning the house and making the perfect meal, the less likely I am to send out those invites. I find that if I stick to a theme, a meal is much easier to execute, and less stress equals a more fun Frances (Jon would agree).

Since we live in the New York area, we have access to amazing fresh bagels. Not much is easier than arranging some bagels and schmears on a platter and adding some lox and fresh fruit. Voilà, bagel brunch! I like the added protein and satisfaction of my Cheddar and Thyme Mini Frittatas (p. 100). Folks can add them to their bagel sandwich or enjoy them on their own.

As the school year comes to a close, there are always plenty of championship games and tournaments. I'll be real with you—I have never been big on team sports. I ran track and swam on my school's swim team, but I'm really an individual athlete. Put me on a ski slope or a dance floor and I'm happy. Jon, on the other hand, loves team sports and credits playing football and baseball with teaching him basic principles like teamwork and the importance of showing up. So even if your kiddo doesn't win the championship, treat them like the champion they are and make my Berry Protein Mini Smoothies (p. 102). They provide brain power to athletes and mathletes alike.

As you'll read in the next section, summer is the most popular season for babies to be born. That means there are tons of baby showers in the springtime in anticipation of all the new arrivals. If you're hosting a shower for a friend, coworker, or family member, it's fun to make a snack tray as part of the celebration. If they've revealed the baby's sex, you can create a tray that's pink or blue, or go gender neutral with a light sage, yellow, blush, oatmeal, or white color scheme.

> So even if your kiddo doesn't win the championship, treat them like the champion they are.

Spring can sometimes feel like just a prelude to summer, but it's my favorite time of year. The weather hasn't gotten too hot, and the bugs haven't come out in droves. Plus, friends haven't taken off for summer travels yet, so they're able to gather for impromptu celebrations. I encourage you to pick a snack tray from the list above, put some beverages in the cooler, and enjoy some quality time with the folks you care about.

MEMORIAL DAY BURGER TRAY

Spend a little time the night before the holiday assembling the slaw to make it easy to throw this tray together. If you're planning to serve both traditional and plant-based burgers, I recommend placing the cooked burgers on separate serving trays and adding little signs so that guests can easily grab the right patty.

- Celebration Slaw (featured recipe)
- Burgers (regular and/or plant-based)
- Burger buns
- Red onion slices
- Cheese slices for cheeseburgers
- Cornichons
- Tomato slices
- Avocado slices
- Ketchup
- Mustard
- Potato chips
- Arugula or romaine leaves
- Crispy onions (such as French's)

Celebration Slaw

Makes 6 servings.

I love a good slaw, but I prefer a light, vinegary one instead of gloppy, mayo-based slaw. This one is bright, crunchy, and delicious on its own, atop a burger, or tossed with noodles.

4 cups shredded red cabbage (1 head)
1 medium yellow or orange bell pepper, seeded and diced
1 cup shredded carrots
1 cup chopped cilantro leaves
2 tablespoons apple cider vinegar
1½ tablespoons extra-virgin olive oil
1½ tablespoons Dijon mustard
1 teaspoon honey
3 tablespoons freshly squeezed orange juice
¼ teaspoon salt
¼ teaspoon black pepper
¼ cup chopped roasted peanuts

1 Toss the cabbage, diced pepper, carrots, and cilantro together in a large bowl.

2 In a separate small bowl, whisk the vinegar, oil, mustard, honey, orange juice, salt, and pepper.

3 Add the dressing to the cabbage mixture and toss. Chill for 20 minutes. Top with peanuts and serve.

ICE CREAM SOCIAL TRAY

The biggest tip I have for this tray is to bring out the ice cream at the very last minute! Or invest in an insulated ice cream container, which will allow you to keep the ice cream out as long as the socializing is going on.

- Homemade Caramel Sauce (featured recipe)
- Ice cream
- Whipped cream
- Chopped walnuts or nuts of choice
- Mini marshmallows
- Halved strawberries

- Bananas
- Cookie dough pieces (Look for the pasteurized ones from Ben & Jerry's.)
- Chocolate sauce
- Sugar cone pieces
- Peanuts
- Chocolate chips

- M&M's or other candy-covered chocolate
- Sprinkles
- Coconut chips or shreds
- Maraschino cherries (The ones from Luxardo are amazing.)
- Chopped peanut butter cups

Homemade Caramel Sauce

Makes one 8-ounce jar.

My kids like store-bought caramel sauce. Me, not so much. It's way too sweet and never has the right amount of saltiness. Homemade caramel sauce does take a certain amount of finesse to make, but it's incredibly satisfying and keeps for a month, which makes it worth the investment in my book.

1 cup sugar
¼ cup water
6 tablespoons unsalted butter, room temperature
½ cup heavy cream, room temperature
1 teaspoon vanilla extract
⅛ teaspoon sea salt

1 Heat sugar and water in a heavy saucepan over medium heat. Stir frequently for 2 to 3 minutes, until sugar melts and mixture turns clear and bubbly, then begin to swirl the pan.

2 Continue to swirl the pan, but don't stir the mixture. Sugar will start to turn gold in about 8 to 12 minutes. Mixture will thicken and begin to look honey colored.

3 Add the butter and stir. If the mixture starts to spit and pop, turn off the heat. Once the butter has been incorporated, return the mixture to medium heat and slowly add the cream, whisking the entire time. Remove from heat and stir in the vanilla and salt.

4 The caramel mixture will be fairly thin but can be used warm or hot. Once cooled, pour any remaining caramel into a clean, lidded glass jar and store in the refrigerator for up to one month. The caramel will become deliciously thick. Warm the caramel in the microwave to get it back to sauce consistency, or just lick it off the spoon.

TACO NIGHT TRAY

Taco night is a favorite around our house, and it likely is at yours as well. When you're ready for something a bit more special than a typical Taco Tuesday, it's time to make a Taco Night Tray! If you make tacos weekly, I highly recommend getting a taco holder, which allows you to fill the tacos without the ingredients spilling out. Plus, they look awesome on a platter! You can make the ground turkey in advance and reheat it just before serving.

- Adobo-Spiced Ground Turkey (featured recipe)
- Taco shells
- Jarred salsa
- Blueberry Salsa (see bonus recipes)
- Shredded red cabbage
- Lime wedges
- Radish sticks
- Guacamole
- Sour cream
- Mexican blend cheese
- Low sodium black beans, warmed
- Tortilla chips
- Rice
- Margaritas for the grown-ups! (see bonus recipes)

Adobo-Spiced Ground Turkey

Makes 6 tacos.

This recipe is so simple but incredibly flavorful. If you prefer ground beef, bison, or lamb, those will work just as well.

1 tablespoon olive oil
½ cup chopped yellow onion
1 pound ground turkey, 85% lean
1 teaspoon adobo seasoning (such as Loisa)
1 teaspoon ground cumin
1 package crunchy taco shells

1 Heat oil in a large skillet on medium-high and add onion. Cook until softened, about 2 minutes.

2 Add the turkey to the pan and cook about 8 to 10 minutes until cooked through, breaking up with a spatula.

3 Add the adobo and cumin and stir to distribute evenly. Cook an additional 2 minutes, until turkey is evenly browned. Serve in taco shells.

Blueberry Salsa

Makes 8 servings.

Have you ever had a berry salsa? It's a very fun take on a familiar food, and I love how the sweet and spicy combo helps bring some extra flavor—and fruit—to taco night.

1 pint fresh blueberries, picked through
⅓ medium red onion, diced
¼ cup fresh cilantro leaves, chopped
Juice of a lime
1 small jalapeño, seeded and minced
¼ teaspoon salt

Roughly chop the blueberries and place in a small mixing bowl. Add the remaining ingredients and stir. Serve immediately or refrigerate until ready to serve. Salsa will keep in an airtight container in the refrigerator for up to one day, depending on how ripe the blueberries are.

Stripped-Down Margarita

Makes 1 cocktail.

I don't like premade mixes or a salted rim for my marg—just fresh lime juice and a good quality tequila. You can always add some simple syrup to this to make it sweeter.

1½ ounces tequila blanco
1 ounce fresh lime juice
1 ounce Cointreau or other orange-flavored liqueur
3 ice cubes

1 Place all the ingredients in a cocktail shaker and shake about 20 to 30 seconds, until the outside of the shaker becomes cold.

2 Strain the margarita into a glass. If you prefer it on the rocks, add one or two ice cubes to the glass first. Enjoy!

BAGEL BRUNCH BOARD

The beauty of a bagel board is just how wonderfully relaxing it is for the host. Everything is already out, so what more can be done? The only issue is with toasting the bagels. You can't slice them and pre-toast them because they will get hard very quickly. One option is to bring your toaster to the room where you're eating, and guests can toast their bagels if they want to. Or you can heat the bagels whole on a baking sheet in a 375°F oven for 5 to 6 minutes. Then just slice in half and serve!

- Cheddar and Thyme Mini Frittatas (featured recipe)
- Bagels
- Cream cheese (regular and scallion or your favorite)
- Lox
- Capers
- Cheddar cheese slices
- Red onion slices
- Green grapes
- Lemon slices
- Tomato slices
- Turkey bacon
- Fresh dill
- Avocado slices
- Jam of choice

Cheddar and Thyme Mini Frittatas

Makes 12 frittatas.

What's better than a bagel with cream cheese? A bagel with cream cheese *and* a savory frittata! Brunch is one of my favorite meals to make. I love pretty much all brunchy foods, *and* I like that I can knock out two meals at one time. Since I want my family and guests to feel satisfied after the meal, I always make sure to include a few sources of protein, like these frittatas, on the brunch tray.

Cooking spray
8 large or 10 medium eggs
1 cup shredded sharp cheddar cheese
¾ cup whole milk
¼ teaspoon sea salt
¼ teaspoon black pepper
2 teaspoons fresh thyme leaves (from about 4 sprigs)

1 Preheat oven to 350°F. Spray a 12-cup muffin pan with cooking spray.

2 Whisk the eggs in a large mixing bowl. Add the cheese, milk, salt, and pepper, and whisk again. Add the thyme.

3 Transfer mixture to a container with a spout (such as a large measuring cup) and pour into the prepared muffin cups, leaving a little room at the top of each.

4 Bake 28 minutes, or until the tops of the frittatas are golden. Let them cool slightly before serving. Frittatas can be kept in an airtight container in the refrigerator for three days or frozen for up to three months.

CHAMPIONSHIP TRAY

Whether you serve up this winning tray on the field or at home, it's sure to score top points. All the items travel well, with the exception of the smoothie. You can either blend it before you head out and transport it in a lidded container or blend it on the spot with a portable, battery-operated blender.

- Berry Protein Mini Smoothies (featured recipe)
- Orange wedges
- Chocolate milk
- Rice Krispies Treats
- Cheese crackers (such as Goldfish)

- Caramel popcorn
- Fruit gummies
- Snack cheese (such as The Laughing Cow)
- Packaged hard-boiled eggs, halved

Berry Protein Mini Smoothies

Makes 4 (½ cup) servings.

This smoothie is one of Leo's favorites. It's perfect for busy school mornings as well as after sports. The protein powder will help repair any microtears that may have occurred in muscles during a game, and it will also help satisfy your ravenous athletes.

1 cup oat milk or milk of choice
1 banana
½ cup frozen raspberries
½ cup frozen blueberries
½ cup frozen strawberries
1 scoop vanilla protein powder, whey or plant-based
3 ice cubes

In a blender, combine milk, banana, frozen berries, protein powder, and ice. Blend until smooth and serve.

BABY SHOWER PLATTER

This delightful tray is fun to prepare and eat. You can make the chia puddings a day in advance. If transporting, make sure to use jars with lids. Cut out the bread for the onesie sandwiches last because it will dry out after an hour or so.

- Mini Dragon Fruit and Chia Puddings (featured recipe)
- Meringues
- French macarons
- Colorful marshmallows
- Pink gummy candy

- Watermelon baby feet and baby bottles
- Cucumber and Brie onesie sandwiches
- Pastel Jordan almonds
- Pink M&M's
- Pink cake bites

Mini Dragon Fruit and Chia Puddings

Makes 5 servings. (Use 5 small jars or glasses.)

FOR PUDDING:

¾ cup chia seeds
3 cups refrigerated coconut milk
1 tablespoon maple syrup
1 teaspoon vanilla extract

FOR TOPPING:

1 cup frozen dragon fruit (such as Pitaya Foods)
1 tablespoon maple syrup
1 tablespoon fresh lemon juice
Zest from 1 lemon

1 In a medium bowl, combine the chia seeds, coconut milk, 1 tablespoon of maple syrup, and vanilla. Set aside.

2 In a blender or food processor, combine the dragon fruit, 1 tablespoon of maple syrup, lemon juice, and zest until smooth.

3 Fill each jar about three-fourths of the way with the chia mixture. Top each with about 2 tablespoons of the dragon fruit puree. Cover and refrigerate at least an hour, or until set. Serve with small spoons.

summer

Summer Rituals 108

Savor Every Day 120

SUMMER RITUALS

When I was a twentysomething website editor living in Washington, DC, I started making weekend trips to the farmer's market on my bike. I didn't grow up in a place that had farmer's markets, so I was charmed by the whole experience: getting there, buying coffee, perusing the various offerings from mid-Atlantic farmers, and finally investing my hard-earned money in some locally sourced produce. These days, we make trips to the farmer's markets in the river towns along the Hudson with the kids and Latke in tow. It's always been super important to me that my kids—and children in general—are able to make the connection between the hard work that goes into growing our food and the meals that end up on our plates. It's much harder to waste food when you think about the time and effort that went into producing that ear of corn or that nectarine.

If you're like me, you go through phases where you're just not very inspired to cook. I experienced this in a significant way during the COVID-19 pandemic. I think I had just gotten tired of all the cooking and cleanup I had to do during that time, and all I wanted to do was go to a restaurant and have someone else make food for me. Sound familiar? For me, the antidote to cooking fatigue is always a trip to the farmer's market. It never ceases to inspire me to make *something*. And of course, summer is an especially enticing season, with the fragrant ripe peaches, glossy cherries, and crisp radishes. The good news is that you can basically gather up all this glorious produce, grab a loaf of good bread and some cheese, put it on a platter, and call it dinner. Want extra credit? Make my Individual Peach Crumbles (p. 110), which are so good and easy to make.

Since school goes until the very end of June here in New York State, the Fourth of July is the first time the kids feel like they're on vacation. Our town puts on a fantastic fireworks display at night, so we fuel up beforehand with a tray that is dedicated to everything red, white, and blue and has lots of star shapes.

The Fourth is also a great time to put that grill to use and make something that's light and healthy, like my Grilled Shrimp and Cherry Tomato Skewers (p. 112).

When the heat starts to build in midsummer, I look forward to nights in the AC with a glass of wine, my favorite people, and a fun movie. The hardest part is finding a film we can all agree on! But the rest is easy. Phoebe is a popcorn monster and somehow manages to eat more than the rest of us combined. Microwave popcorn is great, but when you want to kick things up a little, try my Kettle Corn recipe (p. 114), which goes well with virtually every movie treat, from Milk Duds to Twizzlers.

My family has had a cabin on a small pond for over fifty years. Growing up, I used to bring friends there for overnights, and we always had s'mores. I had to twist my mom's arm to buy the milk chocolate, marshmallows, and graham crackers because she didn't normally buy those ingredients, but she saw how happy my girlfriends and I were, roasting marshmallows and occasionally getting them stuck in each other's hair!

Today my own family is lucky enough to have a firepit in our backyard, which lends itself to impromptu s'mores nights. I love coming up with new and creative ways to make a s'more, like adding a layer of peanut or chocolate-hazelnut butter to the graham cracker or adding a few banana slices to the middle. And we recently tried using saltines instead of graham crackers for a less-sweet version—so good!

> It's important to me that my kids make the connection between the hard work that goes into growing our food and the meals that end up on our plates.

After a long, carefree summer, Labor Day can feel like a downer. Our school system starts up just after the holiday, so the celebration takes on a "last hurrah" vibe. I tend to lean into that and make a snack tray to celebrate all that's wonderful about summer—juicy watermelon, sweet corn with toppings, potato salad, and burgers. It's my way of sending summer off on a high note while helping my kiddos wrap their brains around starting a brand-new school year.

FARMER'S MARKET BOARD

I've featured my family's market faves on this board, but you can let them serve as suggestions. The beauty of shopping at the farmer's market is that you never know what you'll be bringing home in your basket.

- Individual Peach Crumbles (featured recipe)
- Blueberries
- Sweet cherries
- Carrots
- Cherry tomatoes
- Sugar snap peas
- Baguette
- Cheese

Individual Peach Crumbles

Makes 6 crumbles. (Use 6 oven-safe ramekins.)

Peaches are a true seasonal pleasure. And there is nothing like the fragrance of a sun-kissed peach on a summer's day. I usually go a little overboard on buying them when they first come into season, so I use the slightly soft ones to make a crumble. These mini crumbles are delicious on their own, or you can add a scoop of vanilla ice cream for true perfection!

FOR FILLING:

5 ripe but firm peaches, sliced (I like a mix of white and regular.)
½ cup fresh lemon juice
1–2 teaspoons lemon zest
¼ cup sugar
½ teaspoon ground cinnamon
1 teaspoon vanilla extract

FOR TOPPING:

¼ cup roasted pecans or almonds, finely chopped
½ cup brown sugar, packed
¾ cup all-purpose flour
¼ teaspoon salt
½ teaspoon ground cinnamon
6 tablespoons unsalted butter, softened

1 Preheat oven to 375°F.

2 In a medium bowl, toss the peaches with the lemon juice, zest, sugar, ½ teaspoon of cinnamon, and vanilla.

3 Place ¾ cup of the peach mixture into each of the ramekins and set aside.

4 In a separate medium bowl, combine the nuts, brown sugar, flour, salt, ½ teaspoon of cinnamon, and butter. Mix with clean hands.

5 Top the ramekins with ¼ cup of the crumb topping and bake 30 to 35 minutes, until bubbling. Serve crumbles hot, or let cool then refrigerate for up to one day before serving.

FOURTH OF JULY TRAY

You can skip the fondant stars on the peanut butter cups, but they do add a colorful, patriotic element. They're quite easy to make too: Simply roll out the packaged fondant with a rolling pin to about one-eighth-inch thickness, then cut out the star shapes with a cookie cutter and gently press them onto the tops of the cups.

- Grilled Shrimp and Cherry Tomato Skewers (featured recipe)
- Cupcakes with star sprinkles and American flags
- Red, white, and blue potato chips

- Red, white, and blue M&M's
- Watermelon, cut into stars
- White chocolate peanut butter cups (such as Justin's) with red and blue fondant stars

Grilled Shrimp and Cherry Tomato Skewers

Makes 10 skewers.

Shrimp is one of my favorite foods to make because it cooks so quickly. That means I can get my seafood fix in record time. This recipe does require a 30-minute marinating time, but it's worth it for the Fourth of July.

10 (10- or 12-inch) wooden skewers
2 tablespoons extra-virgin olive oil
¼ teaspoon salt
¼ teaspoon black pepper
¼ teaspoon ground cumin
¼ teaspoon ground aji amarillo, optional
¼ teaspoon chili powder
1 tablespoon fresh thyme leaves (from about 6 sprigs)
2 garlic cloves, minced
1 pound cleaned and deveined shrimp
2 pints cherry tomatoes

1 Soak the skewers in water for 30 minutes (a large baking dish works well for this). Place oil, salt, pepper, cumin, aji amarillo, chili powder, thyme, and garlic in a zip-top plastic bag. Seal the bag and gently shake to combine. Add the shrimp and tomatoes, seal the bag, and then massage the outside of it to make sure each shrimp gets coated with marinade. Refrigerate for 30 minutes.

2 Thread 3 shrimp and 3 tomatoes onto each skewer in an alternating pattern. Discard marinade and bag.

3 Heat a grill or grill pan on medium-high. Add the skewers and cook 2 to 3 minutes per side, or until the shrimp are opaque. Remove from grill and serve. Assist younger children with removing shrimp and tomatoes from skewers.

MOVIE NIGHT SNACKS

Not only is this a fun way to level up movie night at home, it's also a fantastic way to save money! I'm sure I don't need to tell you that movie theaters mark up the cost of popcorn and candy by several hundred percent, making a trip to the theater a costly event. Popcorn and candy are musts, but it's nice to include a snack with a little more substance, like nachos. We like to top ours with queso, sliced olives, and jalapeños, but you can top yours however you like.

- Kettle Corn (featured recipe)
- Twizzlers
- Milk Duds
- Dots
- Gummy bears
- Butterfinger candy bars
- Junior Mints
- Good & Plenty candies
- Nachos
- M&M's or other candy-coated chocolate pieces

Kettle Corn

Makes about 15 cups.

We've always eaten a lot of popcorn at our house, but it wasn't until the pandemic that I tried making kettle corn. It's not difficult, but it's certainly nuanced. If you end up burning some kernels the first time, do not be discouraged! Depending on your pan, the kernels, and the intensity of your burners, you may need to adjust the directions a little. But the end result is absolutely delicious and 100% worth it! Be sure to use a kitchen towel to hold the handle of the lid while you're shaking the pan because it will be hot.

Note: If serving to younger kids, look through the popped corn and remove any unpopped kernels. Also, kids under four should not be served popcorn.

¼ cup avocado oil or other vegetable oil
½ cup popcorn kernels
2 tablespoons sugar
¼ teaspoon sea salt

1 Line a baking sheet with parchment paper and set aside.

2 In a large, deep saucepan with a lid, add the oil and a few of the kernels. Cover the saucepan and bring the heat up to high (if you're using a power burner, heat just to medium).

3 Once you hear the kernels pop, add the remaining corn to the hot pan. Add the sugar and salt on top, replace the lid, and shake the pan. The popping will become steady. Continue shaking the pan until there's a pause in popping.

4 Remove the pan from the heat and pour the popcorn onto the baking sheet. The popcorn will be hot! Wait a minute or so before transferring it into single-serving containers.

S'MORES BOARD

I do love to enjoy s'mores around the fire, but if you don't have a firepit or fireplace, don't let that stop you! You can easily microwave s'mores for about 30 to 45 seconds to achieve the same deliciously melty result.

- Mini Chocolate PB Cups (featured recipe)
- Chocolate bars
- Marshmallows
- Sprinkles
- Graham crackers (regular and chocolate or cinnamon)

- Saltine crackers
- York Peppermint Patties
- Peanut butter
- Chocolate-hazelnut spread
- Fruit and marshmallow skewers (We like to use watermelon, cantaloupe, green grapes, and raspberries.)

Mini Chocolate PB Cups

Makes 18 cups.

S'mores are always fun, even at their most basic—chocolate, marshmallow, and graham cracker. But when you really want to impress folks, add some homemade peanut butter cups. They are quite easy to make, only require three ingredients, and are a wonderful substitute for a piece of milk chocolate, especially when the chocolate and peanut butter start mingling with the melted marshmallow—heavenly!

1½ cups semisweet chocolate chips, divided
1 tablespoon plus 1 teaspoon coconut oil, room temperature
½ cup creamy peanut butter

1 Place 18 mini paper baking cups on a parchment-lined baking sheet.

2 In a small, microwave-safe bowl, place 1 cup of the chocolate chips and 1 teaspoon of the coconut oil. Heat in the microwave for 1 minute. Stir with a spatula until the chocolate is completely melted. If necessary, continue heating in 30-second increments until chocolate is completely melted and smooth.

3 Pour about 2 teaspoons of the chocolate into each paper cup. Place in freezer for 10 minutes. (Keep the bowl handy that you used for melting—you'll be using it again.)

4 Meanwhile, combine the peanut butter and remaining coconut oil in a medium bowl. Remove the cups from the freezer and spoon 1 tablespoon of the peanut butter mixture into each cup.

5 In the same bowl you used earlier, heat the remaining chocolate chips in the microwave for 1 minute. Stir until the chocolate is smooth. Pour about 1 teaspoon of the chocolate on top of the peanut butter cups.

6 Place cups in freezer for 30 minutes, until solid. If you're using these for a s'mores tray, arrange other items on the tray first, then add the peanut butter cups to prevent them from melting too much.

LABOR DAY TRAY

You're likely already grilling up some burgers or hot dogs for Labor Day, so why not put them on a festive tray? I've included a few of my favorite corn-on-the-cob toppings, but feel free to add anything else you'd like.

- Red, White, and Blue Potato Salad (featured recipe)
- Corn on the cob
- Spicy mayo
- Unsalted butter, melted
- Crumbled feta cheese
- Watermelon wedges
- Burgers and buns
- Mustard
- Ketchup
- Relish

Red, White, and Blue Potato Salad

Makes 12 servings.

This potato salad is similar to one my mother used to make. She always found mayo-based American-style potato salad to be a little heavy, so she made hers with oil and mustard instead. I love the tanginess of the dressing and the colors of the potatoes. If you have leftovers, they go well over some arugula or baby spinach.

3 pounds red, white, and blue new
   potatoes
¼ cup extra-virgin olive oil
¼ teaspoon salt
3 tablespoons whole grain Dijon mustard
2 tablespoons white vinegar
2 tablespoons fresh lemon juice
1 tablespoon fresh thyme leaves (from
   about 6 sprigs)

1 Place the potatoes in a large stock pot and fill with water an inch above the potatoes. Bring to a boil and cook 20 minutes. Drain.

2 Meanwhile, combine the oil, salt, mustard, vinegar, lemon juice, and thyme in a large bowl. Add the hot potatoes to the oil mixture and toss. Once they're cool enough to handle, slice the potatoes in half with a paring knife and toss again. Serve immediately, or cover and refrigerate until ready to serve.

SAVOR EVERY DAY

When we lived in Brooklyn, Jon and I planned date nights regularly. We had a reliable babysitter, and there were hundreds of restaurants and bars for us to explore in the area. Then the pandemic hit, we moved out of the city, and we went for a nearly two-year stretch without going anywhere, just the two of us. But just because we couldn't leave our kids behind didn't mean we couldn't take a virtual trip to Greece or Spain. If you can't find a sitter, or the budget isn't there this month for a nice restaurant, I highly recommend making my Date Night Mezze Platter. There's something luxurious about having lots of little bowls of flavorful ingredients at your fingertips, leisurely enjoying them with a glass of wine, and not having to cut up your child's chicken or pick up strands of pasta from the floor. If possible, find a kid-friendly movie, set up your children with water bottles and age-appropriate snacks, and find a quiet spot in your house (within earshot of the kids) or on your porch where you and your partner can simply enjoy each other's company plus a nice wedge of Manchego cheese.

Each summer, our two older kids, Willa and Leo, look forward to going to sleepaway camp for a couple of weeks. They get to enjoy a boatload of fun activities, and Jon and I get to enjoy having fewer responsibilities. It's a win-win! But I know the kids get a little nervous before they leave (new kids, new counselors), so we carve out some time the week before camp to check in with them and let them know we're here if they have any questions or concerns before they leave the nest. And offering some camp-themed treats, like Puffed Rice Campfire Treats (p. 124), always takes the edge off.

Whether you're welcoming home your campers or your college students, it's always nice to have some homemade treats ready and waiting. I remember when my older brothers and sister would return from college or military training and my mom would make their favorite meal. It made me jealous at the time, but I get it now. When you've been away from home, it doesn't matter how fabulous your time away was, you're still going to miss certain comforts of home. My Welcome Home Tray consists of family faves, like stuffed olives, chips and salsa, salami, and cheddar, as well as my Macaroon Brownies (p. 126), which will definitely help show how much you missed your kid.

> Whether you're welcoming home your campers or your college students, it's always nice to have some homemade treats ready and waiting.

Statistically speaking, in the United States, more babies are born in the summer than during the other seasons. This could be because those summer babies were made during the coldest months of the year when people are more likely to engage in indoor activities. Whatever the reason, there are more birthdays to celebrate from July through September. When you want to put together a little birthday fete without throwing a full-on party, a snack tray is a great way to go. Make my Chocolate Cupcakes with Vanilla Buttercream Frosting (p. 128), pair them with other fun treats, add some party hats, put on Kidz Bop, and you've got a fun time!

DATE NIGHT MEZZE PLATTER

In my opinion, everything goes with a dry rosé. Pretty much anything from Provence fits the bill, but I especially like Whispering Angel or Avaline, which is organic. Here's hoping you and your sweetie can linger for a while over this romantic board.

- Classic Creamy Hummus (featured recipe)
- Pistachios
- Walnuts
- Manchego cheese
- Pita bread
- Stuffed olives
- Extra-virgin olive oil for dipping
- Fig jam
- Baba ghanoush (eggplant dip)
- Cucumber spears
- Harissa (spice paste that can be added to hummus)

Classic Creamy Hummus

Makes 1½ cups.

Mezze (or meze or mezzeh) is a Middle Eastern style of eating that involves shared dishes or small plates that can make up an entire meal. A common food that is served as part of mezze is hummus, that garbanzo bean dip that Americans just can't get enough of. I love this creamy and not-too-garlicky version and make it often. Don't skip cooking the chickpeas in the baking soda—that's what helps soften them, allowing the hummus to blend up silky smooth.

1 (15-ounce) can chickpeas, rinsed and drained
½ teaspoon baking soda
¼ cup fresh lemon juice
⅓ cup tahini
¼ teaspoon salt
1 tablespoon extra-virgin olive oil, plus more for drizzling
1 garlic clove, finely chopped
2 tablespoons cold water
Cracked pepper, optional

1 Place chickpeas in a medium saucepan, add the baking soda, and fill with water an inch above the chickpeas. Bring to a boil, then reduce heat and simmer 20 minutes until the chickpeas are very soft. Drain remaining water and rinse with cold water.

2 Transfer the chickpeas to a blender or food processor. Add the lemon juice, tahini, salt, oil, and garlic, and blend. The mixture will be very thick. Add the water a little at a time until the hummus is fully blended and creamy.

3 To serve, transfer hummus to a serving bowl, drizzle with olive oil, and sprinkle with a little cracked pepper if you'd like. Add the hummus to your mezze platter and enjoy!

SUMMER CAMP SEND-OFF SNACKS

As with a few of the other trays, I recommend filling this out with your kid's favorite snacks. You know, the ones they beg you to send to them at camp.

- Puffed Rice Campfire Treats (featured recipe)
- Cucumber spears
- Sandwich cookies
- Yogurt-covered pretzels
- Soft pretzel bites (such as Pretzilla)
- Sweet cherries
- Trail mix
- S'mores (These can be made in the microwave.)

Puffed Rice Campfire Treats

Makes several treats, depending on size of cookie cutter.

Before you say that you can't decorate to save your life, let me stop you. You can, because these are really easy! If you can use a cookie cutter and a tube of toothpaste, I guarantee you can add flames to these puffed rice treats. The decorating icing comes in a pouch, and it's really easy to squeeze out—promise! I found my campfire cookie cutter on Amazon.

Cooking spray
3 tablespoons unsalted butter
1 (10-ounce) package marshmallows
6 cups puffed rice cereal
Orange decorating icing (such as Wilton)
Semisweet chocolate chips

1 Spray a 9 × 13-inch baking dish with cooking spray.

2 In a large saucepan, melt the butter over low heat. Add the marshmallows and stir until fully melted. Remove from heat.

3 Stir in the cereal until it is fully coated with marshmallow and transfer to the prepared dish.

4 Spray a spatula with cooking spray and press down on the cereal mixture until even. Use a campfire cookie cutter to cut out shapes.

5 Use decorating icing to fill in the campfire flames. Press the pointed ends of the chocolate chips into the rice treat in an X pattern to resemble logs.

WELCOME HOME TRAY

When you haven't seen your child in weeks or months, such as a college-bound kid, there's a lot of catching up to do. This tray makes it easy to put the focus on communication instead of food prep because everything can be done in advance. If possible, make the brownies a day ahead and slice up the watermelon then too. Then set everything out and enjoy the reunion.

- Macaroon Brownies (featured recipe)
- Watermelon slices
- Pimento-stuffed olives
- Cheddar cheese
- Salami slices
- Chocolate-covered pretzels
- Trail mix
- Tortilla chips
- Salsa
- Dried persimmon slices or other dried fruit
- Cherry tomatoes
- Belgian waffles/stroopwafels

Macaroon Brownies

Makes 20 brownies.

Brownies are awesome all on their own, but I'm a big fan of all things coconut, so when I saw that my friend Jake Cohen had included coconut macaroon brownies in his book *Jew-ish*, I had to come up with my own slightly easier version. These do not disappoint!

1 (18-ounce) box brownie mix (such as Ghirardelli Double Chocolate)
3 egg whites
¼ teaspoon salt
½ cup sugar
1 teaspoon vanilla extract
2 cups unsweetened shredded coconut

1 Preheat oven to 325°F. Lightly butter and flour an 8 × 8-inch baking pan.

2 Make brownies according to package but remove from oven 10 minutes earlier than suggested.

3 Meanwhile, place egg whites and salt in a large mixing bowl or in the bowl of a stand mixer. Using a hand mixer or stand mixer, whip eggs on high for about 3 minutes, until stiff peaks form. With mixer running, add in sugar and vanilla.

4 Increase oven temperature to 350°F. Place the coconut in a separate bowl. Fold in the whipped egg mixture. Using a spatula, evenly spread the coconut mixture over the brownies.

5 Bake 30 minutes, until top is golden and brownies are set. Allow to cool completely before cutting.

HAPPY BIRTHDAY BOARD

Birthdays are all about making the birthday kid (or adult) feel special. Look for treats and decorations in any theme they love.

- Chocolate Cupcakes with Vanilla Buttercream Frosting (featured recipe)
- Mini ice cream cones
- Ice cream
- Lollipops (such as YumEarth)
- Animal cookies (such as Mother's Mythical Creatures)
- Stuffed marshmallows with sprinkles (such as Stuffed Puffs)
- Candy-coated milk-chocolate gems (such as UnReal)

Chocolate Cupcakes

Makes 12 cupcakes.

Cooking spray
1½ cups all-purpose flour
¼ cup whole wheat flour
1 cup sugar
½ cup plus 2 tablespoons unsweetened cocoa powder
1 teaspoon baking powder
¾ teaspoon baking soda
¼ teaspoon salt
1 cup buttermilk or whole milk, room temperature
¼ cup extra-virgin olive oil
1 large egg, room temperature and beaten
1 teaspoon vanilla extract
½ cup boiling water

1 Preheat oven to 350°F. Line a 12-cup muffin tin with liners. Spray liners with cooking spray.

2 In a large bowl, combine dry ingredients with a spatula, making sure to break up any clumps.

3 In a separate bowl, whisk together the milk, oil, egg, and vanilla. Add this mixture to the dry ingredients and combine in a stand mixer or with a hand mixer. Carefully add the boiling water in two parts and stir to combine. Don't splash yourself!

4 Fill cupcake liners about three-fourths full. Bake 20 minutes, or until tops are dry. Cool completely before frosting.

VANILLA BUTTERCREAM FROSTING

I use cream cheese in my buttercream because my kids prefer a cream cheese frosting—and a not-too-sweet one—but I like to frost cupcakes with buttercream. Our compromise is this deliciously creamy one.

8 ounces (1 block) plain cream cheese, softened slightly
½ cup (1 stick) unsalted butter, softened slightly
1¼ cups powdered sugar
Pinch salt
2 teaspoons vanilla extract
Sprinkles, optional

1 In a medium mixing bowl, beat the cream cheese and butter until smooth. Add the sugar in two parts, beating until incorporated. Add the salt and vanilla and beat again for 1 minute.

2 If the frosting is too soft, cover and refrigerate 20 to 30 minutes, until firmer. Transfer frosting to a disposable piping bag. Snip off the end and pipe frosting onto the tops of the cupcakes. Top with sprinkles if desired.

fall

Fall Feels 132

Welcome Friends! 144

Celebrate the Harvest 156

FALL FEELS

When I was a kid, I despised fall. That crisp air and the reddish tinge on the maple trees, which started in late August, always signaled the end of fun for me. With such long, cold winters in western New York's snowbelt, I hated the thought of summer's carefree days ending.

Motherhood has given me an entirely new perspective on fall. I love our relaxed summer days spent swimming, scootering, and grilling, but I'm always pretty ready when it's time to break in the new school backpacks. The kids inevitably feel a mixture of nerves and excitement over which classes they'll be in and whether they'll still get to sit next to their best friend. I always take the classic "first day of school" photos, which my kids are now old enough to hate doing. But they know when they come home from school on that first day, they'll be greeted with a hug and an extra-fun First Day of School Snack Tray.

Since the first day of school always tends to be on one of those gorgeously sunny September days, I like to include as much end-of-summer fruit as possible. And I always make grilled cheese sandwiches in the shape of each kid's initial to make them feel special. Leo loved these as a little guy and still does as a middle schooler. To cool the kids off, I include a small bucket of ice to serve popsicles in.

I've come to love our "fall things," like picking out pumpkins, spending an afternoon putting spiderwebs on the front of the house, and debating the best placement for the plastic bats and skeletons on the front lawn. Halloween is one of my favorite holidays. I enjoy helping the kids come up with a plan for their costumes and getting them ready for a night of trick-or-treating. We like to build the excitement in the weeks leading up to Halloween by watching all the kid-friendly classics, like *Room on the Broom*, *Hocus Pocus*, *The Addams Family*, and now *Wednesday*.

There's an overabundance of candy on Halloween night, so I like to fuel up the ghouls and goblins with a Halloween snack tray that's fruit forward and provides plenty of protein. Since I know my kids will be getting lots of sugar later in the night, I make sure I set them up with balanced snacks that will keep them satisfied and energized while we're out trick-or-treating. This means a mix of things like mandarin jack-o'-lanterns, guacamole, and my wickedly fun Fright Night Fruit Skewers (p. 138).

Like clockwork, about a month into the school year, what begins as a totally smooth start to the semester seems to take a U-turn and someone comes home very upset over a test score, a fallout with a friend, or an embarrassing classroom situation. I remember how these things felt as if they happened to me yesterday! It's so painful to feel like you're not part of the friend group or that you're falling behind in class. When these moments happen, it's time for a heart-to-heart with your kid. And in my house, it's also time for a snack tray made just for that child.

While food shouldn't be used as an emotional crutch or a reward, it's true that favorite foods can soothe us when we're feeling down. Use my Tough Day at School Tray as a jumping-off point for your own kiddo on those terrible, horrible, no good, very bad days. Since you don't know when to expect them, just do a quick rummage through the cupboard and fridge and see what favorite foods you can come up with. Help smooth out those rough edges with an individual snack tray that's just for your kiddo. If it's hard to get them to share what happened at school, you might want to include happy-face, sad-face, and neutral-face stickers so they can point to the emotion they're feeling. You can also provide a small notepad and pencil so your child can write down how they feel if that works better for them. Then sit down, put your phone away, and put your listening ears on.

> Motherhood has given me an entirely new perspective on fall.

Once those bumps get smoothed out and the school year is humming along, I start getting requests for sleepovers. My daughters are five years apart and have totally different styles and personalities, but that's what makes their relationship so special. Willa, the oldest kid, is pragmatic and loves a good murder mystery. Phoebe, the youngest, adores Hello Kitty and kawaii, which is the Japanese term for all things cute.

When my daughters have begged me long enough, I relent and agree to a sleepover. I love having their friends stay over, but I never get much sleep. We often let Willa and Phoebe have sleepovers on the same night to avoid losing sleep twice. I ask them what their friends like, and we come up with a snack tray that has a little something for everyone. Since the two groups split up after dinner, this is one of those occasions where I provide plates for guests to put their selections on instead of letting them just nibble from the tray. One thing I've learned—don't put too much chocolate on a sleepover snack tray unless you want everyone staying up well past midnight!

> Help smooth out those rough edges with an individual snack tray that's just for your kiddo.

As my kids get older, I'm learning to help them navigate the awkward things we all go through as well as the new challenges that have come from technology and changing social norms. It's quite simple to soothe a toddler with a scraped knee, but helping your tween get past a rude comment or a social media put-down is quite another. Even though my heart breaks a little because they don't need me like they used to, trust me—they *still* need me. And I love that a little time spent on my part, cutting up some veggies and cheese and making sure I've included something for everyone, still brings them running to see what's on the snack tray.

FIRST DAY OF SCHOOL SNACK TRAY

Make that first day special with this fun tray. If your kids don't like grilled cheese, you can easily make their initials from peanut butter and jelly sandwiches using letter-shaped cookie cutters. The cheese flowers are made with a flower-shaped cookie cutter and white and yellow cheddar.

- Apple "Donut" Rounds (featured recipe)
- Pineapple star wands
- Cucumber spears
- Grilled cheese initial sandwiches
- Soft pretzel bites (such as Pretzilla)

- Ice pops on ice
- Applesauce pouches
- Puffed snacks (such as Pirate's Booty)
- Cheese flowers
- Additional fruit (such as berries or melon)

Apple "Donut" Rounds

Makes 6 to 7 donut rounds.

Donuts have never been my favorite. I have nothing against them—they're just not my jam. But I do enjoy these apple "donuts," or fauxnuts—whatever you'd like to call them. They're quite fun and super easy to make, plus you can top them with whatever you like.

1 Fuji apple, cored and sliced into 6 or 7 rounds
3½ tablespoons smooth peanut or almond butter
3 teaspoons jam
⅓ cup sprinkles

1 Pat tops of apple rounds dry with a paper towel and spread about 1½ teaspoons of the nut butter onto each round.

2 Top half of the donut rounds with jam.

3 Place the sprinkles on a plate. Place remaining apple rounds face down into sprinkles. Transfer rounds to snack tray and serve.

SPOOKY HALLOWEEN SPREAD

It's time for some frighteningly tasty snacks! Gather your little monsters and have them help assemble the skewers and draw faces on the mandarin oranges. If they're four or older, they can also help add candy eyes to just about anything. Just add a bit of honey or nut butter to the back of the eyes to get them to stick. This spread is perfect for an at-home monster mash or a school celebration.

- Fright Night Fruit Skewers (featured recipe)
- Black and orange tortilla chips (such as Xochitl)
- Guacamole
- Vanilla mochi with "mummy frosting" and eyes
- Pretzel rods with white chocolate and festive sprinkles
- Mandarin jack-o'-lanterns (Use a Sharpie to draw faces on unpeeled oranges.)
- Black licorice rounds or whips
- Popcorn hand (We used hand-shaped treat bags from Wilton.)
- Wax-wrapped snack cheese with monster faces (We used Mini Babybel.)
- Cauldron filled with hummus or dip of choice

Fright Night Fruit Skewers

Makes 8 skewers.

Halloween is definitely when my crafty side comes out! I hope you and your ghouls unleash your creative beast too when you make these spooky skewers. Look for skewers that are pointy only on one end, and help little ones slide the fruit and marshmallows onto them.

8 firm kiwifruits
1 medium cantaloupe or honeydew melon
8 large marshmallows (such as jumbo Jet-Puffed)
8 (8- or 10-inch) wooden skewers
Candy eyes
Edible ink pen (such as Bakerpan)
Honey or nut butter (to attach eyes)

1 Peel the kiwis, slice in half widthwise, and set aside. Line a baking sheet with paper towels.

2 Cut the melon in half; scoop out and discard the seeds. Use an ice cream scoop to scoop out 8 melon rounds and set aside.

3 Blot all the fruit with paper towels. On the baking sheet, assemble the fruit-and-marshmallow skewers in whatever order you like. You can alternate kiwi, marshmallow, and melon on each skewer, or do skewers with all kiwi, all marshmallow, or all melon.

4 Use honey or nut butter to attach the candy eyes to the fruit. Use the edible ink pen to draw faces on the marshmallows. Carefully transfer skewers to snack tray and let the goblins gobble them up!

TOUGH DAY AT SCHOOL TRAY

The truth is that this tray isn't really about the food. It's about getting your kid to open up about whatever upsetting thing happened that day. The cookies are a plus, but you can also simply use their favorite snacks and whatever helps them feel safe and relaxed.

- Oatmeal Chocolate Chip Cookies (featured recipe)
- Blueberries or other favorite fruit
- Hershey's Kisses
- Emoji stickers or small notepad and pencil
- Favorite stuffy
- Milk or other beverage

Oatmeal Chocolate Chip Cookies

Makes about 27 to 30 small cookies.

These satisfying little cookies have just the right amount of sweetness from a combination of brown sugar and dates. I like that they're a little bit chewy and include whole grain oats.

6 tablespoons unsalted butter
½ cup packed light brown sugar
1½ cups rolled oats
⅓ cup all-purpose flour
⅓ cup whole wheat flour
¾ teaspoon baking soda
½ teaspoon salt
2 large eggs, beaten
1 teaspoon vanilla extract
1 cup pitted dates, chopped
½ cup semisweet chocolate chunks or chocolate chips

1 Preheat oven to 350°F. Line two baking sheets with parchment paper or silicone baking mats.

2 Melt the butter in a small saucepan over low heat. Remove from heat and stir in the brown sugar.

3 Combine the oats, flours, baking soda, and salt in a medium mixing bowl. Stir the butter mixture into the dry ingredients. Add the eggs, vanilla, dates, and chocolate chunks or chips and combine well.

4 If the mixture starts to fall apart, place it in the refrigerator for 15 minutes. Using 2 spoons, transfer dough by tablespoonfuls onto prepared baking sheets. Bake for 12 minutes, or until the tops are dry to the touch. Cool on a wire rack before serving.

SLEEPOVER SNACK TRAY

Whether your kids and their friends are playing board games or watching a movie, this tray is ready to fuel the festivities. If you have several kids staying over, use a marker to add each child's name to their paper plate so they don't get them mixed up.

- No-Bake Cereal Bars (featured recipe)
- Mandarin oranges (such as Halos)
- Carrots, preferably multicolored
- Ranch dressing
- Chocolate-covered pretzels with sprinkles
- Gummy worms
- Chocolate chip cookies
- Popcorn
- Tortilla chips

No-Bake Cereal Bars

Makes 24 bars.

A sleepover tray should provide enough food so that your kids don't come asking for another meal after dinner. I like to include a hearty mix of classic salty snacks, like pretzels, popcorn, and tortilla chips, with fruit, veggies, and a smattering of gummy worms (they'll love you for it!). And I always include these No-Bake Cereal Bars, which are like the ones your mom used to make, just a wee bit healthier.

Cooking spray
2 cups rolled oats
4 cups Honey Nut Chex cereal
¾ cup honey
½ cup brown sugar
1 teaspoon vanilla extract
2 tablespoons unsalted butter or plant butter
1 cup creamy peanut butter
Pinch salt
2 cups semisweet chocolate chips
¼ cup hemp seeds
Sea salt for sprinkling on top, optional

1 Spray a 9 × 13-inch baking dish with cooking spray and set aside. In a large mixing bowl, combine the oats and cereal; set aside.

2 In a medium saucepan, bring the honey and sugar to a boil. Turn down the heat and simmer 5 minutes. Stir in the vanilla and butter and whisk until the butter melts. Add the peanut butter and salt and whisk until fully incorporated. Remove from heat.

3 Pour the peanut butter mixture over the oat-cereal mixture and combine with a spatula until fully coated. Transfer the mixture to the prepared pan.

4 Melt the chocolate until smooth in a double boiler on the stove or in a microwave-safe bowl for 1½ minutes (it may need more time). Stir in the hemp seeds. Pour the chocolate over the cereal mixture, spreading evenly with a spatula to the edge. Sprinkle sea salt over the top, if using.

5 Cover dish with foil or beeswax wrap and refrigerate for at least one hour. Cut into 24 bars and serve. Bars can be stored, covered, in the refrigerator for up to five days.

WELCOME FRIENDS!

Kids of all ages can have playdates, but once they're about ten, they don't want you to call it that anymore. Instead, it's "hanging out," but hangouts require snacks too. I always like to check in with the parents prior to the play-date to make sure I can accommodate any food allergies or preferences. And although we're keeping it easy and not producing elaborate trays, it's nice to include a few fun items as conversation starters, especially when young kids are just getting to know each other. Next to the snack tray you could put down some kraft or drawing paper, along with some crayons. Or add some small toys to play with.

My friends and family know that I don't really care about football, even though my husband used to play. But that doesn't stop me from wanting to celebrate on game day. I grew up near Buffalo, New York, so you can bet there were tons of spicy wings served at every tailgate party I ever attended. As a vegetarian in high school, I wasn't left with much to eat except the celery. That's why I love the concept of cauliflower wings (p. 148). True, cauliflower doesn't actually have wings, but the florets are pretty satisfying when you bread them, coat them with buffalo sauce, and bake them. So good!

Have you ever met new neighbors and then told them to "drop by any time" for drinks and snacks? Most folks won't just drop in on you these days, but every once in a while, it does happen. Or maybe a friend or relative texts to let you know they are in the area and just want to pop over. Instead of letting anxiety take over, put your partner and kids on cleanup duty and go see what's in the freezer. You likely have a pizza and maybe some apps on hand. Throw those in the oven pronto! Then put some nuts in a bowl, grab any cheese and veggies you have, and start assembling. Add my Avocado

Goat Cheese Emergency Dip (p. 150), chill some juice boxes and vino, and you're all set.

Does your family do Meatless Monday? This global campaign started in 2003 and encourages people to eat less meat and include more plants in their diet to improve their health and the health of our planet. While our household is omnivorous, we have been reducing our meat consumption over the past few years, and I continue to incorporate more plant-based meals into the rotation.

> Offering a vegetarian or vegan dish in the context of a tray can be a low-stress way to introduce new options to your family.

If you've been trying to get your family to reduce their meat consumption too, you know it can be challenging. Offering a vegetarian or vegan dish in the context of a tray can be a low-stress way to introduce new options to your family. If you offer them foods they're familiar with, like hummus, bread, rice, and sweet potato fries, they'll be more likely to give new foods, like Chickpea and Quinoa Patties (p. 152), a try. And even if they don't try them the first time, don't get discouraged. It can take up to fifteen exposures for a kid to try a new food. So keep at it! And keep modeling the behavior you want to see.

PLAYDATE SNACKS

This particular snack tray is designed for kids ages four to five, and all the items are presented in a way that is safe for them to handle on their own. But it can also be enjoyed by children of all ages. Young kids don't necessarily want to stop playing while they're eating, so it's fun to put some kraft paper on your table and let them doodle while they snack.

- Veggie Cups with Ranch Dressing (featured recipe)
- Cheddar crackers (such as Goldfish Colors)
- Apple slices
- Fig bars (such as Nature's Bakery)
- Yogurt-covered pretzels
- Pretzels
- Animal crackers (such as Mother's Mythical Beasts)
- Fruit snacks
- Quartered grapes (for kids four and under; older kids can eat them whole)

Veggie Cups with Ranch Dressing

Makes 8 servings (1 cup of dressing).

Since kids are more likely to eat their veggies when they're presented with dip, I created a delicious, creamy version of ranch dressing.

1 garlic clove
1 cup mayonnaise (I like Primal Kitchen's avocado oil version.)
¼ cup plain kefir
1 tablespoon white vinegar
¾ teaspoon Worcestershire sauce
¼ teaspoon sea salt
1 tablespoon fresh dill
2 tablespoons fresh chives
¼ teaspoon dried parsley
Baby carrots, halved, or carrot chips
2 small zucchini, quartered
Jicama, peeled and cut into sticks

1 Place the garlic on a cutting board and use the flat side of the blade of a chef's knife to smash it. Remove the papery skin and mince.

2 In a blender or food processor, combine the garlic, mayonnaise, kefir, vinegar, Worcestershire sauce, salt, dill, chives, and parsley. Blend on high until smooth and light green. Chill before serving.

3 Assemble veggie cups by pouring 2 tablespoons of dressing into small cups or ramekins. Add veggies and serve.

TAILGATE TRAY

If you're a fan of chicken wings, feel free to add them to this tray. And if you end up serving regular *and* vegan blue cheese dressing, just add a little sign to designate which is which.

- Buffalo Cauliflower Bites (featured recipe)
- Blue cheese dressing
- Stuffed mushrooms
- Pizza, cut into small wedges
- Guacamole
- Cucumber spears

- Cherry tomatoes
- Baby bell peppers
- Baby carrots
- Hummus or other bean dip
- Potato and/or tortilla chips
- Cheese, cubed

- Chocolate chip cookies
- Mini peanut butter cups
- Yogurt-covered pretzels or yogurt-covered almonds
- M&M's in the colors of your favorite team (Yes, I'm a Bills fan!)

Buffalo Cauliflower Bites

Makes 6 servings.

Even if you love chicken wings, I encourage you to give these vegan cauliflower bites a go. They have the same satisfying flavor as wings, without the chicken or the mess.

¾ cup almond flour
1 teaspoon smoked paprika
1 teaspoon garlic powder
½ teaspoon salt
¾ cup unsweetened almond or oat milk
1 head cauliflower, cut into florets
½ cup vegan buffalo sauce (such as Primal Kitchen)
Blue cheese dressing (regular or vegan), optional

1 Preheat oven to 425°F. Line a baking sheet with parchment paper.

2 In a large mixing bowl, combine the flour, paprika, garlic powder, salt, and milk. Add the cauliflower florets and toss to coat.

3 Transfer the cauliflower to the baking sheet and bake 20 minutes, flipping halfway through.

4 Remove the baking sheet from the oven and brush cauliflower with the buffalo sauce. Return to the oven for 15 minutes, or until the florets are tender and the edges have darkened. Place cauliflower bites on your tray and enjoy!

NEIGHBORS ARE COMING TRAY

If you end up making this tray when people are dropping by unexpectedly, my advice is to cut the food into bite-size pieces and make it look as abundant as possible (even if you haven't been to the store in days). And always taste test that half-empty bag of chips or nuts to make sure they're still fresh!

- Avocado Goat Cheese Emergency Dip (featured recipe)
- Frozen pizza, cut into bite-size pieces

- Cucumbers
- Carrots
- Veggie chips
- Almonds

- Cheese, sliced into wedges
- Any frozen appetizer you have on hand
- Any sweet treat you have on hand

Avocado Goat Cheese Emergency Dip

When you're a food person, people like to throw you a challenge now and again. I went to a conference where we had a *Chopped* type of competition and had to come up with a recipe out of the ingredients that were on hand. I saw some perfect avocados and grabbed them! But I didn't want to make just guacamole, so I grabbed some goat cheese too. The resulting combo was surprisingly delicious, nabbed me second place, and now is something that's officially in the Roth rotation. I've noted substitutions in case you need them.

4 ounces plain goat cheese or cream cheese
1 avocado, pitted, or 1 cup cooked and shelled edamame
Juice of a lime
¼ teaspoon salt
¼ teaspoon black pepper
½ jalapeño, seeded and minced, or ½ teaspoon crushed red pepper flakes

1 Place the cheese in a medium mixing bowl. Add the avocado or edamame, lime juice, salt, and pepper, and either mix with an electric hand mixer or mash with a large fork.

2 Stir in the jalapeño or pepper flakes. Taste and adjust seasonings if necessary.

MEATLESS MONDAY TRAY

If you haven't tried za'atar, get ready to be obsessed! This combo of dried herbs (marjoram and thyme), sesame seeds, sumac, and salt is delicious on everything from hummus to potatoes to roasted lamb.

- Chickpea and Quinoa Patties (featured recipe)
- Tzatziki
- Pistachios
- Tabouleh
- Olives
- Naan
- Shepherd's Salad (see bonus recipe)
- Hummus
- Za'atar
- Frozen sweet potato fries (such as Alexia)
- Brown rice

Chickpea and Quinoa Patties

Makes 12 patties.

Not only are chickpeas a great source of protein and fiber, they also contain their own egg replacer. The liquid they're canned in is called aquafaba, and it can be beaten just like eggs and used in desserts and recipes like this one.

3 cups water, divided
Pinch salt
1 cup quinoa, rinsed
4 tablespoons extra-virgin olive oil, divided
2 garlic cloves, minced
1 teaspoon ground curry
1 teaspoon ground ginger
1 teaspoon ground cumin
½ teaspoon salt
1 (15-ounce) can chickpeas, drained and rinsed (reserve liquid!)
3 tablespoons all-purpose flour

1 Bring 2 cups water with a pinch of salt to a boil and add quinoa. Turn heat down to medium-high, cover, and cook 10 to 15 minutes until water is absorbed. Remove from heat, stir, cover again, and let it steam for 5 minutes. Let the quinoa cool to room temperature.

2 In a separate saucepan, heat 2 tablespoons oil over medium heat. Add garlic, curry, ginger, cumin, and ½ teaspoon salt. Cook 2 to 3 minutes, until garlic is golden. Add chickpeas and remaining 1 cup water, and simmer 10 minutes, or until chickpeas are tender. Remove from heat and let cool. Using a potato masher or a large fork, mash chickpeas until mostly smashed, but leave a few chunks.

3 In the meantime, transfer the reserved chickpea liquid (about 1 cup) to a medium bowl and beat with an electric hand mixer on high for 2 to 3 minutes, until white and frothy.

4 When the quinoa and chickpeas have cooled slightly, combine them in a large bowl. Fold in the whipped liquid and flour, and chill 15 to 20 minutes.

5 In a large skillet, heat 1½ tablespoons olive oil on medium-high. Form patties out of the quinoa and chickpea mixture ¼ cup at a time. Transfer patties to hot skillet and cook 5 minutes per side, or until golden. Add remaining ½ tablespoon oil to pan and cook remaining patties. Serve hot.

Shepherd's Salad

This type of salad is served throughout the Mediterranean, from Greece to Turkey to Israel. It is very refreshing and easy to put together, and it works well with both grilled meats and vegetarian dishes. And yes, most kids love it!

1 large greenhouse cucumber, diced
2 plum tomatoes, seeded and diced
½ cup feta cheese, cut into chunks
¼ cup red onion, diced
1 tablespoon extra-virgin olive oil
¼ teaspoon salt
2 tablespoons fresh lemon juice

Combine all the ingredients in a medium bowl. Serve immediately or refrigerate until ready to serve.

CELEBRATE THE HARVEST

I grew up near a town called Ellicottville in western New York. It's a special little village that's home to the Holiday Valley Ski Resort as well as charming shops and many festivals, including their Fall Fest. As a kid and teen, I remember tramping through the wet leaves to look at all the crafts for sale, hoping my mom would let me buy a new ring or pair of earrings. The weather was often a little chillier than I'd planned for, and the cup of hot cider we would buy was an absolute necessity. There were often big, fluffy pumpkin muffins for sale too, and their cinnamon-spice flavor always stuck with me. I've come close to re-creating that taste and texture in the Ginger Pumpkin Muffins (p. 158) on the Fall Fest Tray.

About once a month in my household, there's a night when I haven't done the grocery shopping or I'm trying to clear out the fridge because we're heading out of town. The kids may say there's no food in the house, but every mom knows there's plenty—you just have to go on a little treasure hunt to find it. We always have some frozen breakfast sausages kicking around the freezer. Sometimes there's even a package of cinnamon rolls in the fridge that I had planned to make the previous weekend but didn't get around to it. And there are always eggs, so I'll whip up a giant omelet for everyone. If I have frozen broccoli or corn, that goes in too. And any leftover wedge of cheese is fair game. Voilà, breakfast for dinner!

Around the holidays, it's wonderful to have a house full of guests, but it can also be really hectic. Pancakes are a crowd-pleaser, but traditional pancakes require the cook to stay at their station in the kitchen until everyone has been fed. While I love a big stack of pancakes, I figured out a few years ago that there's a better way to serve them to a crowd—and all you need is a sheet pan (see recipe on p. 162). When you bake pancakes in a sheet pan, it frees you up to do other things, like catch up with your sister-in-law or finally order your holiday cards.

Thanksgiving is one of my favorite holidays because you can celebrate it no matter what your religious affiliation or your country of origin. Thanksgiving in my house is less about tradition and more about gathering together to appreciate one another and give thanks for the bounty of the season. We often serve a roast turkey, but not always since it's not everyone's favorite. However, we do always serve a fruit-based creation, which I call Tessa the Turkey. If you're looking for a fun food craft to keep your kids and maybe your mom busy, I highly recommend putting one together! I'm also a big fan of turkey-themed craft kits with googly eyes, and I'll happily make those with anyone who is game.

> Thanksgiving is one of my favorite holidays because you can celebrate it no matter what your religious affiliation or your country of origin.

Whether you celebrate or start to hibernate when the first chilly fall day arrives, I hope you find some new ways in this chapter to embrace the season. For me fall is always a time of reflection, and it's when I start thinking about personal goals that I want to focus on in the coming year and ways to spend quality time with my family. Will we take the same summer trip as usual or try a new adventure? Maybe we'll finally take that trip to Europe so the kids can try a real croissant and I can show them my mom's hometown. If *Everyday Snack Tray* has helped spark special moments in your home, that would fill my heart with joy and mean I've accomplished what I set out to do.

With love and gratitude,
Frances

FALL FEST TRAY

Whether you're serving this tray outside or inside, the best way to keep the cider warm until your guests are ready to enjoy it is to transfer it to a thermos or a slow cooker. Feel free to add mulling spices or rum to the cider—just keep it separate from the one for the kids!

- Ginger Pumpkin Muffins (featured recipe)
- Hot apple cider
- Donut holes
- Apple slices
- Pear slices
- Red grapes
- Fresh pomegranate
- Candied nuts
- Cheese
- Pain d'epi (French wheat-stalk bread) or baguette

Ginger Pumpkin Muffins

Makes 12 muffins.

Cooking spray
1 (15-ounce) can pumpkin
2 large eggs, beaten
½ cup pure maple syrup
½ cup (1 stick) unsalted butter, melted and slightly cooled
½ cup crystallized ginger, chopped, plus 2 tablespoons sliced
1 cup all-purpose flour
1 cup whole wheat flour
¼ cup chia seeds
¼ teaspoon baking powder
1 teaspoon baking soda
¼ teaspoon salt
¼ teaspoon ground cardamom
¼ teaspoon ground cloves
½ teaspoon ground cinnamon

1 Preheat oven to 375°F. Line a 12-cup muffin pan with liners. Spray liners with cooking spray.

2 In a mixing bowl, combine the pumpkin, eggs, maple syrup, butter, and chopped ginger (reserve sliced ginger for later).

3 In a separate bowl, whisk together the flours, chia seeds, baking powder, baking soda, salt, and spices. Add the wet ingredients to the dry and mix well.

4 Scoop ⅓ cup of the mixture into each muffin liner. Add a few pieces of the sliced ginger to the top of each.

5 Bake 20 minutes, or until tops of muffins are dry to the touch. Let cool and place on snack tray. Muffins can be stored up to five days in an airtight container in the refrigerator.

BREAKFAST FOR DINNER PLATTER

As a lover of all things breakfast, I could literally eat breakfast foods for every meal of the day. Luckily for me, the star of many breakfast dishes—eggs—are enjoyed by the whole family. Turn them into a satisfying veggie omelet, grab whatever you can find to round out the platter, and you've got dinner.

- Broccoli-Cheddar Omelet (featured recipe)
- Bagels, English muffins, or toast
- Berries or other fruit
- Packaged hard-boiled eggs, quartered and sprinkled with "everything" bagel seasoning
- Cream cheese
- Butter
- Breakfast sausage (regular or plant-based)
- Cinnamon rolls
- Arugula or baby spinach

Broccoli-Cheddar Omelet

Makes 6 servings.

The beautiful thing about an omelet is that it's endlessly versatile. You can fill it with any type of cheese, meat, herb, mushroom, or veggie, and it will always taste amazing. The hardest part is not overcooking or undercooking the eggs, so a little patience is required to get it just right.

1 cup frozen broccoli florets
6 large eggs, room temperature
¼ cup milk of choice
¼ teaspoon salt
¼ teaspoon pepper
½ teaspoon unsalted butter
½ cup shredded cheddar cheese (or whatever cheese you have on hand)

1 Microwave the broccoli according to package directions. Drain any water and set the broccoli aside.

2 In a large bowl, whisk the eggs with the milk, salt, and pepper.

3 In a large skillet, melt the butter over medium heat; add the egg mixture. Turn down heat slightly. Cook 4 minutes, then add veggies and cheese to one side of the eggs. Fold in half and cook an additional 2 to 4 minutes, until edges are set. Transfer to a cutting board, slice into 6 pieces, and serve.

PANCAKE BREAKFAST BOARD

If you've never done a swirl pattern on a baked good, don't stress—it's easy! It's quite simple to do with a toothpick and has no impact on the flavor of the pancakes. If you're setting these out as a grab and go, it's nice to provide small paper bags and napkins.

- Berry-Swirl Sheet-Pan Protein Pancakes (featured recipe)
- Bacon
- Blueberries
- Strawberries
- Maple syrup
- Walnuts
- Butter
- Chocolate-hazelnut spread
- Peanut butter
- Whipped cream
- Jam
- Mini chocolate chips

Berry-Swirl Sheet-Pan Protein Pancakes

Makes 15 servings.

If your kids have early morning practice, it can be tough to send them out the door with a hearty, protein-rich breakfast. I love these pancakes because they contain added protein from the buttermilk and the protein powder, plus they're portable.

FOR PANCAKES:

Cooking spray
2 cups buttermilk
2 large eggs, beaten
1 teaspoon vanilla extract
4 tablespoons unsalted butter, melted
⅓ cup pure maple syrup
1¼ cups whole wheat flour
1 cup all-purpose flour
¼ cup vanilla protein powder
1 teaspoon baking soda
2 teaspoons baking powder
½ teaspoon sea salt

FOR SWIRL:

1 cup strawberries, fresh or frozen and thawed
½ cup raspberries, fresh or frozen and thawed
1 tablespoon fresh lemon juice
Powdered sugar, for topping

1 Preheat oven to 425°F. Line a rimmed 11 × 17-inch sheet pan with parchment paper. Spray parchment with cooking spray.

2 Whisk the buttermilk, eggs, vanilla, butter, and maple syrup together in a medium mixing bowl; set aside.

3 In a separate mixing bowl, combine the flours, protein powder, baking soda, baking powder, and salt. Add the wet ingredients in two to three additions to the dry and combine well.

4 Pour the pancake mixture onto the prepared sheet.

5 In a blender, combine the berries with the lemon juice and blend until smooth. Evenly space dollops of the puree onto the pancake mixture (make 5 rows of 3 dollops). Starting in the upper right corner of the pan, use a toothpick to drag the puree through the mixture in an "S" pattern.

6 Bake 11 minutes. Let cool and sprinkle with powdered sugar. Using a pizza cutter or a knife, cut into 15 squares. Transfer to tray and serve. Leftover pancakes can be stored in an airtight container in the refrigerator for two days.

THANKSGIVING TRAY: TESSA THE TURKEY

This snack tray is quite different from all the rest in *Everyday Snack Tray*. It's not an assortment of seasonal bites; it's just one big edible presentation. I've been making a variation of Tessa the Turkey for several years now. I started making her when I realized I needed something to keep my kids busy at the children's table on Thanksgiving while the grown-ups were having appetizers and cocktails. Tessa has turned into a holiday tradition and never fails to bring a smile to everyone's faces. And she's a turkey that everyone can eat!

1 firm pear, preferably red Anjou or Starkrimson, halved, with stem removed
1 cup red grapes
1 cup green grapes
2 star fruits, sliced
1 cup dried apricots
1 cup goldenberries (also called Cape gooseberry or husk cherry)
1 cup cubed mango
1 cup fresh cranberries
1 cup raspberries
10 (8- to 10-inch) wooden skewers
2 candy eyes
Honey
Orange peel (just the colorful part) cut into shapes of turkey feet, wattle, and beak

1 On a large platter, place a pear half, cut side down, in the middle of the platter. Snack on the remaining half or use elsewhere.

2 Thread the fruit onto the skewers in a rainbow pattern, starting with the red grapes and ending with the raspberries. Once you've assembled the skewers, poke the pointy ends into the side of the pear, leaving a little room between each one.

3 Attach the candy eyes and the orange-peel wattle and beak to the pear with a little honey. Arrange the orange-peel feet on the platter, just under the pear. Introduce Tessa to your guests!

Cranberry Dip

If you're from the midwestern United States, you've likely had some version of this cranberry dip at a family or community gathering. It's often made a little spicy with jalapeños, and sometimes the cranberries are used raw. It's always served over cream cheese. Since this dip is meant for the whole family, I've skipped the peppers and cooked the berries into a sauce. And since I'm not a midwesterner, I like using goat cheese instead of cream cheese—but you go with what your crew likes! Serve with your favorite sturdy crackers.

2 cups cranberries, fresh or frozen and thawed
¼ cup packed brown sugar
½ cup water
Zest of an orange
2 tablespoons fresh orange juice
½ teaspoon ground cinnamon
4 ounces plain goat cheese or block-style cream cheese

1 In a medium saucepan, bring the cranberries, brown sugar, water, orange zest, orange juice, and cinnamon to a boil. Stir and reduce heat to medium. Simmer for 10 minutes, until berries pop and the mixture thickens. Remove from heat and allow to cool slightly.

2 Place goat cheese or cream cheese in a serving dish and top with the cranberry sauce.

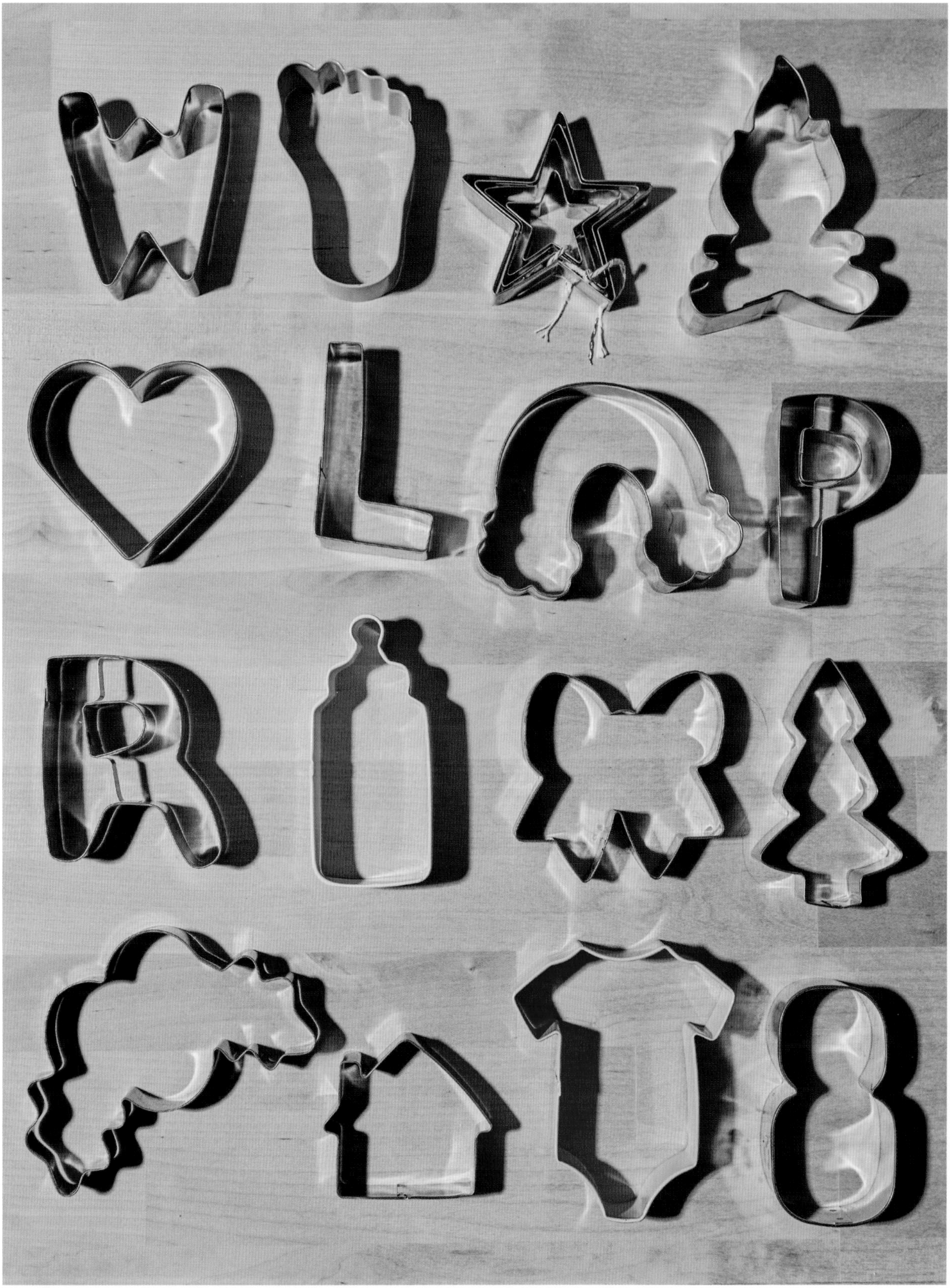

Acknowledgments

When you write a book, going from concept to finished work always takes a leap of faith. And there is no way I could have pulled this off without the massive support of the wonderful team at Revell. Huge thanks to Kelsey Bowen for believing in my vision and getting as excited about snack trays as I am. And to Kristin Adkinson for her sharp eye and deft editing skills.

To my team at ARC Collective—Shab, Joyce, Brooklyn, Markie, and Taylor—thank you for always sharing your enthusiasm for my ideas and for helping me take them to the next level.

To Lauren Volo, Maeve Sheridan, Mira Evnine, Micah Morton, Megan Litt, and Sheelagh Regan, thank you for making this book look as inviting and delicious as the snack trays I create in my dreams. Maeve, you somehow found the most perfect trays to elevate Mira's expertly styled snacks to another level. And those birch logs! Lauren, I feel like we've been talking about motherhood and work-life balance for at least a decade, and it means so much to me to bring this book to fruition with you behind the lens. You went the extra mile, and it absolutely shows in these pages. And a special shout out to Monica Pierini, who couldn't be there for the shoot but who made absolutely sure we received all of our ingredients, especially the peaches.

To Rocky Owens for producing the lifestyle shoot. You managed to co-ordinate five wardrobe changes and keep everyone on track and in a good mood, including Latke the doxie.

To Emily Amick for settling my nerves and making me and the whole Roth squad look "just right" and as lovely as possible. To Ruth Do Rosario at The

Beauty Parlor for hiding those grays, which popped out more than ever during the making of this book. And to Johanna Sapakie for helping me get strong so I could lift and carry all those snack-laden trays.

To Justin's, Stuffed Puffs, YumEarth, USA Pears, Vosges Chocolates, Wonderful Pistachios, and Zespri for sending all the amazingly yummy products for the shoot. To Spindrift and Kate's Real Food for keeping our energy up, and to Pendleton for sending such a lovely blanket to make our fireplace scene extra cozy.

To my sister, Liz, who has always supported me and who helped me remember all the wonderful German foods our mom used to make.

And last but most definitely not least, to Leslie Stoker for believing in me and my ideas when others just didn't get it. And for holding my hand through so many milestones.

On the last studio day with the Dream Team; *from left*, Ashleigh Sorbone, Megan Litt, Maeve Sheridan, Mira Evnine, me, and Lauren Volo

Resources

Bakerpan

Edible pens and cookie cutters

BakerPan.com

Fancy Sprinkles

Fun sprinkles and edible glitter

FancySprinkles.com

Justin's

Nut butter and nut butter cups

Justins.com

Loisa

Modern Latin cooking ingredients, like adobo

Loisa.com

Luxardo cherries

The best maraschino cherries out there

Williams-Sonoma.com

Meri Meri

Whimsical cupcake toppers and decor

MeriMeri.com

SmartSweets

Low-sugar candy options

SmartSweets.com

Stroopwafels

Belgian-style waffle cookies

RipVan or Jacquet

RipVan.com

JacquetBakery.com

Stuffed Puffs

Fun, stuffed marshmallows covered in sprinkles

StuffedPuffs.com

Supernatural

Artificial-dye-free and vegan sprinkles, food colors, baking chips, and
frosting mix

SupernaturalKitchen.com

Unreal

Traditional chocolate candy, made with less sugar

UnrealSnacks.com

Wilton

Candy eyes, frosting, monster snack bags, and baking supplies

Wilton.com

YumEarth

Allergen-free and vegan candy

YumEarth.com

Recipe Index

FRANCES LARGEMAN-ROTH

Frances Largeman-Roth is a registered dietitian nutritionist, *New York Times* bestselling author, and nationally recognized nutrition and wellness expert. A member of the James Beard Foundation and the Academy of Nutrition and Dietetics, Frances is a contributor to several publications, including Today.com, *Parents*, and *Parade*, and has appeared on numerous national TV shows, including the *Today* show, the *Rachael Ray* show, *Good Morning America*, QVC, and CNN. She is a proponent of a balanced, plant-forward lifestyle and loves helping people make healthy eating fun. She lives with her husband, their three kids, and their doxie, Latke, in Dobbs Ferry, New York. To learn more, visit her website, www.FrancesLargemanRoth.com, or follow her on Facebook @Frances.LargemanRoth, Instagram @FrancesLRothRD, or Twitter @FrancesLRothRD.